OVER-SEXED AND UNDER-LOVED
A Recovery Guide to Sex Addiction

Douglas H. Ruben, Ph.D.

First Edition

Writers Club Press
San Jose New York Lincoln Shanghai

Over-Sexed and Under-Loved
A Recovery Guide to Sex Addiction

All Rights Reserved © 2000 by Douglas H. Ruben

No part of this book may be reproduced or transmitted in any form or by any means, graphic, electronic, or mechanical, including photocopying, recording, taping, or by any information storage or retrieval system, without the permission in writing from the publisher.

Published by Writers Club Press
an imprint of iUniverse.com, Inc.

For information address:
iUniverse.com, Inc.
620 North 48th Street
Suite 201
Lincoln, NE 68504-3467
www.iuniverse.com

Library of Congress Cataloguing-in-Publication Data

Ruben, Douglas
Over-Sexed and Under-Loved by Douglas Ruben, Ph.D.
1. Addiction Treatment: Sex
2. Sexual Addiction

ISBN: 0-595-09137-7

Printed in the United States of America

Contents

Words of Hope vii
 But you can...

Chapter One 1
Start Your New Life Today
 Why Yesterday is Gone
 Why Mistakes are Okay
 Look Ahead Two Steps at a Time
 Pride has a new Face
 Just Do, Don't Say You'll Do

Chapter Two 21
Why Bad Habits Linger
 Feels Right
 Others Say It's Right
 Scared to Change
 Stupid is What Stupid Feels
 I "Gotta" Do It
 Then What Happens?

Chapter Three 37
Defuse the Habits Now
 Five-step Way to Say "No."

> Three ways others can help you say "No."
> Whoops! No Substitute Habits
> Good Things to Do Instead

Chapter Four..51
Tempted to Give Up?
> It Hurts Too Much
> Others Want Me to do Bad Things
> Life Won't Be Fun
> It's Like Going to Mars

Chapter Five 67
The New You
> How to Like the New You
> Showcase Your Good Points
> Be a Leader, Be a Helper
> Make it Stick

Chapter Six 81
Use Condoms: A Warning about Diseases and Aids

Chapter Seven 87
Can Sex Be Love?

Chapter Eight 93
What Makes a Healthy Partner?
> Type A, B, and C

Chapter Nine 99
What Kind of Lover Are You?

Chapter Ten 105
What Is Great Sex?
Foreplay and Afterplay
Okay "Touch" Areas

About the Author 113
Douglas Ruben

Words of Hope

Urges-that is what I feel. They overwhelm me, and I can't stand them. It's as if a loud voice repeats the message over and over again. "Do it. Do it now." That's what I hear inside my mind. An inner voice screams at the top of its lungs to give in. "Go ahead," it says. "Surrender to temptation."

I listen to that voice. It soothes me. I like what it says. I know how I will feel after I do what the voice says to do—relieved, happy, serene, and fulfilled. Why wait? I don't know why, I prefer not to wait. Believe me. I'd rather give in now.

Often I do. We all do. Urges are everywhere. You have an urge to eat. So you eat. You have the urge to sleep. You sleep. You have the urge to stay home from work and you do it. Yes, you even have the urge to do nothing but vegetate in front of the TV. You give in to that urge, too.

Urges flirt with your subconscious. Your inner ear hears what you'd really like to do. Eat, drink, run around the house naked—anything your heart desires. Picture living out your wildest fantasy all because of an urge. You'd do it if you could, and many of you already have. You're experts at it.

What do urges start with-a need, a physical, maybe an emotional, impulse? You've felt that. You know *something* starts it. You can't escape it. Your body gets signals from all over the place.

Think about it. You first feel pumped with raging excitement and feel driven. All senses point in a straight line to what you want. Urges keep you focused. You can't think about anything else. You can't talk about anything else. Nothing in your body functions except a one-track mind programmed like a missile. It aims at one specific target and has heat sensors to track down that target. The target is to feel good. You've got to feel good.

That's where sex comes in. Sex feels good. It produces pleasure. You relax. You feel calm and finally release those charged electrodes in your body. At last you have relief. Physically your body feels limp. Mentally you lose consciousness. You float in limbo, happy and not really worrying about space and time.

Sex is a tranquilizer for some people, and for others it's an upper. If you think of it as your favorite experience, feeling high or low will depend on how often you get sex. Have sex daily and you experience a steady diet of your favorite feeling. If you lose that frequency, the feeling vanishes. Do it twice a week or once weekly? Forget that! You won't give up the electricity, the instant meditation, the quick fix for your craving.

Okay, once or twice a week is fine for some people. However, not you, you're different. That's why you're reading this book. You know what you like. You know you don't want sex once a week. Not you, ever. Sex doesn't happen that way. On your schedule, sex is frequent—hourly, daily, or minute by minute. For you, the 11th commandment is, "Thou shalt have sex in abundance."

That's your belief.

How you have sex varies. You do it with somebody else or you do it by yourself in bed, in the shower, or somewhere private. You do it with fantasy or pornography. You do it for physical and emotional relief. You do it with persons of any age, any gender, any time, anywhere—it really doesn't matter. You don't care.

What matters is orgasm. You're not picky, just determined. You know what you want and you get it. Like a locomotive you have a place to go and you'll get there with your one-track mind. No turning back; no obstacles block your path. It *will* happen. One way or another, you'll have sex.

Sex is like breathing; you do it all the time. You think about it and talk about it. While looking at people you mentally fantasize you're having sex with them. It doesn't embarrass you to know this; it feels normal. Even the physical sensations feel normal.

Tingling sensations around your thighs happen anywhere. They don't stop. They don't go away because you say, "go away." Sensations are not like pets who will obey when you tell them to leave you alone. Sensations are stubborn. They grow more intense, then overpower your thoughts. You feel sensory jolts rush through your veins. You can't concentrate on anything else. Your body becomes a high voltage wire sending frantic messages of arousal to your mind. Your sensations become unbearable. You can't tolerate it any longer. You don't—you get relief. You have *orgasm*.

Every day the cycle is the same. You get turned-on to the point you can't ignore it. Sure, you try. You pretend you're normal. You look at people and paste on a fake smile. You talk in polite chitchat and disguise your inner sexual feelings. You pretend you're okay, knowing it's a lie. You're not okay, you're fixated, fully plugged into your body's needs. You mentally picture yourself as an overheated engine—hot inside and needing cooling. You're the prisoner of an insatiable craving for an orgasm. It holds onto you as tightly as a Boa Constrictor. It doesn't let go until you make it let go by doing what it wants you to do—produce a climax. Not in two hours; not in five hours; not even later in the day.

The time is now. You want orgasm this minute.

You can't wait. It's uncontrollable. Obsessive thoughts spin faster and faster. Your urge becomes overwhelming. You feel suffocated. All other action stops because you can't think about anything except sex. It's all important. It absorbs you like a powerful vacuum. You are swallowed whole by a whale of arousing physical emotions. You see only one way out of it—succumb to the urge. Don't try to outsmart the urge because it will devour you if you toy with it.

You see no escape from its metal jaws and only one way out of this mess. You do exactly what you've done every other time this has happened. You have sex.

When it's over, you feel good. You can think straight; you can carry on a sane conversation. Your mental images are not about screwing. Your body is not on fire. For an hour or two you experience inner peace and quiet. Yes, amazingly, life returns to normal.

Don't get used to it. Recess is almost over. Periods of calm are short, lasting half an hour, maybe an hour. Relief bought you a little time but you're due for another wave of urges. As soon as your body regenerates its sexual potency, you're in trouble again. You're in sensory flight before you know it, again obsessing over ways you can feed your voracious appetite for sexual stimulation.

Trouble is, you may be getting tired of this cycle. Sure, it was fun at first. You even had a partner who went along with your cravings. They still may be helping you-or are they gone? Now what? Do you satisfy your craving yourself? Masturbate all day long? Been there, done that. Now it's boring. You've sung that tune a million times and can go through the motions blindfolded. Same old, same old.

Excitement is gone. You are no longer doing sex for sex. You're doing it because you can't stop doing it. Your body compels you to do it—you're physically addicted to sex. You're afraid of what will happen if you stop your habit.

But you can...

This book is for you. It will help you stop your habit. *Over-sexed and Under-loved* does not mean you *are* a sex maniac. It means you've made sex an idol. You worship it and you make sacrifices to it. You have made it a measure of whom you are and what you think of yourself—sex is you; you are sex.

If that sounds funny, ask yourself this, "Who am I when I'm not involved in some aspect of sex?"

Good question. Part of you disappeared when sex took over, and sex has been an anchor in your personality for many years. Does that mean sex must vanish before the old me returns? Maybe, but the goal is not celibacy. Sex is as natural as eating. You can regain your identity and still feel alive even with sex. However, there's one catch: Sex has to stop dictating your life.

I know you're thinking, "This is crazy. How can I do this?" Longtime habits don't disappear overnight. You're convinced you'll wake up tomorrow and be driven by the usual forceful sexual needs. It seems intuitive. How can you possibly turn off this act of nature?

Will power won't do it. Nor will any bag of tricks. What it takes is a stronger dose of mental medicine. You'll find the practical tools you need in every chapter you read. Step by step you can follow the hands on approach laid out for you and learn to free yourself of life-inhibiting habits.

Consuming habits can become nonconsuming. A curious mind and a little energy to do some reading are all you need to get started. Begin with Chapter One and see how quickly you can spot yourself. You're headed in the right direction when you recognize you. Believe me, it is a positive direction.

Say "Thank you" to yourself for seeing yourself clearly. You can feel good for nonphysical reasons for the first time in a while.

I know how it feels. I have to say, "Thank you" all the time. I say it to myself to stop all sorts of cravings. I also say, "Thank you" to people who give me healthy direction such as my friends Dr. Charles Keating and Marilyn Osman. Even to my buddy, Joe, I have to say "Thank You." Otherwise, both he and I will slip into paralyzing obsessive traps.

I'd vanish into an abyss of silence where I'd ruminate over sexual fantasies were it not for my wife, Marilyn. She keeps me on track. I have to be on guard with myself to stop the intoxicating effects of old habits. It is 24 hours a day duty. My marriage doesn't save me from slipping back into old habits. I have to do it to save me. It's *my* job. Marilyn is a reminder of what I can do for myself and how I can shape my identity free of compulsion.

You can do it too. The first step is easy. Just read a chapter. Read it tonight. Go ahead, read it now.

Chapter One
Start Your New Life Today

Consider Bob. He's a loner. Sure, he likes to go out occasionally after work. Who doesn't? He has a beer, maybe a mixed drink, and pizza, too. He goes to all sorts of places but mostly bars. Straight bars, gay bars, in between bars—it doesn't really matter—Bob just wants to have fun.

What does he do? It varies. He may sit, nursing his drink, staring at men and women at other tables. That's his favorite hobby, eye-cruising, seeing who's out for a good time. Bob's an expert at people-watching. If he gets bored, he'll ask a bartender or friend the inside gossip on somebody he spots. That's easier than approaching the stranger himself. No way he'd do that. Bob doesn't want to know what the stranger he focuses on really thinks. He wants to *fantasize* what the stranger thinks. It's safer that way.

After an hour or so, Bob makes his move. He waits for the stranger—guy or girl—to notice him. They better or Bob gets angry. Somehow they do. Bob gets lucky. He has the magic touch. People drift toward him. He's like a magnet.

Anyway, they talk. Bob gets the person to open up personally. Like a dentist pulling a tooth, he extracts their deepest, sensitive cavity of personal information.

Bob loves it. The person seems to love it. All seems to be going well as Bob sits there looking at his new companion. However, he's not there at all! He's fantasizing having sex with this individual. Erotica fills his mind. Outwardly he's polite but inwardly he's scheming. He is mentally undressing this person, feeling pangs of sensual excitement. His mind pictures him or her naked and begging for Bob to inflict his virility. Bob loves the feeling. Just thinking about this powerful image keeps him smiling while the two converse.

Nobody knows about his fantasy. It is Bob's secret—his private orgy. He's exploiting it for every dime it's worth.

Inevitably, the fantasy is ruined. The person Bob is speaking to politely excuses himself or herself and walks away. A perfunctory, "Thanks for talking" and off they go. Game over; fantasy ends.

Bob is livid! This person abandoned him. After all, Bob thinks, I cruised this individual all night, wasted my God-damn time until this person noticed me and end up chitchatting for nothing.

Bob feels tricked. He can't believe this person has the nerve to walk away from him. After all, what the hell did he do wrong? He did nothing wrong, absolutely nothing.

Bob tears the person apart in his mind—that little pansy, that little whore. Infuriated by his rejection, he ruminates how horrible this person was and why he or she deserves punishment. Bob hates the individual. He thinks the person is worthless—and wants him even more. Bob's fantasy of sexually wanting this guy heats up but not for passion, for pain. Bob wants to hurt him and make him suffer, thus sadistically proving Bob is superior and that this squirt is a moron.

"Oh, yes, you'll see," Bob repeats to himself, "I'll get you, you son-of-a-bitch."

Okay, Bob, we get the picture. Sex drives your need for approval. If you feel you can score with somebody, bingo—you win. If you can't, it's the death sentence—they lose. Black or white, win or lose, you see no gray and no in-between. You have to feel you're on top—Mr. Bigshot.

You have to be in control. If you don't get your way, it's the other person's fault, right? Right! Blame it on somebody else.

This is what a sex maniac does. He or she doesn't own their lust. They don't even know they have lust. They know just one thing—I want what I want when I want it. Let me have it and I feel okay. Rob me of it and I'll be damned if you get away with it. "Don't screw with me!"

Bob is not an exception. He's the rule. Obsessive? Maybe. A little fanatic? Sure. Yet he's smack dab in the middle of normalcy. Bob's world of make-believe is so real to him that he doesn't know where the exit sign is. He's what happens when sex maniacs lose sight of what they're doing to themselves. When sex-on-the-brain becomes a habit, you respond with animal instincts. You want something, so you get it. Nothing stops you.

That's what Bob did. He cruised the bar. He didn't care what gender he picked. Hell, it didn't matter to him. He just wanted flesh. He fed on his fantasy of getting aroused and deluded himself into thinking reality was like his fantasy.

What he thought is what he did. He imagined having sex with somebody and he really expected to have sex with them. When it happened—great. The fantasy came true. The one-night stand fueled his mental movies.

When the person didn't consent and the fantasy didn't come true, Bob blew up. He let the world know he was angry, angry at the person who didn't fulfill his fantasy.

Whether you think like Bob or are less extreme, it's time to look in the mirror. Look straight into your eyes and ask yourself, "When do I want to stop this emotional roller-coaster?"

I get high when I have sex or think I'm going to have sex; I feel low when I don't have sex or erotic plans get spoiled. Up and down—that's all I do. Same old game. Sure, I change the players, change the scenery; even change the type of sex. Sometimes I do it in the missionary position; sometimes orally; behind; in front; or in a "69" position. I don't really care how the orgasm happens, I just want the high. The method is only a means to an end."

Well, end it.

Make this chapter your first pledge to start over; it's time to stop the vicious, erotic cycle of addiction.

"How," you ask?

"Overnight?"

"Maybe through hypnosis?"

No, I don't think so. Truth is, you won't stop having sex. You'll still do it, probably a lot. What will be different is you'll have sex for the *right reasons*.

So, do yourself a favor and finish reading this chapter. Let your mind go on a field trip for the next half hour. Picture yourself doing what this chapter asks you to do. It's doable. You'll know you're doing it because you're not thinking about sex. You don't believe me? You think you can't budge from cerebral erotica? I'll prove it to you. Read on.

Why Yesterday is Gone

Let's play a game. It's called "forgiveness." Take a moment to think about somebody with whom you wanted to have sex. A girlfriend, boyfriend, husband, wife—it doesn't matter who it is. Just focus on them for the moment. Got a good mental picture of them? Okay.

Now, remember how you felt when they refused you? Angry, right? Big-time rage filled your insides and rushed up your spine? Got it?

Make that feeling come alive. Go ahead— immerse yourself in it. Taste it; smell it; feel hostility bubble up like a volcano about to explode. You can feel the anger, can't you? You feel it inside your muscles, around your chest, in your hands and legs? Out of nowhere it's flooding into your veins. Can you feel it now?

Good. Hold onto it. Don't let go of the feelings. Hold them in. Put a lid on the bottle. Hear your inner voice cursing at those son-of-bitches for rejecting you.

"Damn-them." Say it inside your mind. Hear yourself screaming at them. Feel the hatred grow. Don't stop it. Keep your mind focused on anger. Build it higher and higher—more, more. Keep it going.

Take the anger up a notch. Feel it so painfully you want to cry. Hear yourself shout, "I'll get back at them. By God I swear, I'll make the person pay."

Now, FREEZE.

Don't move. Don't think. Don't breathe.

Take a deep breath, then slowly exhale, blowing air gently through your lips. Do it one more time.

Now take a slow breath of air. Count 1-2-3 as you inhale to keep it slow. Hold that puff of air you inhaled. Hold it, don't let it go. I mean it—hold it for a second or two.

Now, let it out. Slowly. Softly. Exhale to the same count of 1-2-3.

Say loudly to yourself, "I FORGIVE THAT PERSON FOR REJECTING ME."

Say it again—louder. If you're by yourself, say it so you can hear yourself loud and clear.

"I FORGIVE THAT PERSON FOR REJECTING ME."

Now, go back to the breaths. Inhale slowly to the count of 1-2-3. Exhale slowly to the count of 1-2-3. You can do it. You just did it a second ago, now, do it again. It's no big deal. Just repeat what you did. I'll wait.

Turn away from the page while you do it. Then, read the next paragraph. Go ahead. Turn away from the page.

Good, you did it right. See, no big deal. Easy as pie. It will be that easy to do again, with an extra line. So, inhale and exhale to the count of 1-

2-3 and say, "I FORGIVE THAT PERSON FOR REJECTING ME. AND I FORGIVE MYSELF FOR HATING THAT PERSON."

That's right. Recite both statements. What's that? You don't believe what you're saying? You're just going through the motions because I asked you to say the words? You feel like a phony? It doesn't feel natural and if it isn't natural, you won't do it, is that right?

Wrong! It has to feel stupid. It has to feel phony. Want to know why? Here's why—you've never done it before. Change always feels weird. You're changing the way you think. Your mind is used to thinking one way and now you're saying, "Think another way."

Your brain doesn't want to think another way. It's happy mentally doing what you've been doing. Why change a good thing?

It's not a good thing. It's a bad thing. Your habits can fool you. They can trick you into thinking everything is normal. You act so smoothly and routinely you'd think you were genetically engineered to do this. Not so. Habits feel *normal* because change feels *abnormal*.

Talk to heart-attack survivors who undergo bypass surgery. They change their eating and exercise habits really quick after a quadruple bypass. Why? It's better than facing a faster end to their lives. Even so, they feel really odd when they make lifelong changes—but they do it and do it well. Ask my father. He hasn't eaten herring in years. He loved herring. Take my word for it. Sex came second to herring with him.

Now you're going to change.

Say goodbye to anger, fury, and rage. They're history. It's yesterday's headline. Let go of resentment. The sex you got was fine and the sex you lost *was also fine*. No feeling cheated. What's done is done. Turn off the mental tapes and pack them away. Not in a suitcase on the ground—ten feet underground.

If you can't bear to erase your mental tapes forever, be wise. Play them one last time, right now. Turn it on, tune it in, and crank up the volume. Do you hear what you're saying to yourself? No? Hear it now? Turn up the volume; balance the treble and bass. Is it coming in clearly?

Sure it is. It goes something like this. "You fool, you've been had! Damn this evil world for robbing me of happiness!"

You've done it. You fried your brain one last time. Your inner voice spilled its guts on a platter and shouted obscenities until it made you feel whole again. Now you can erase its angry message permanently. Just push the erase button in your brain. You can do it. Say "I don't need to be angry just because I don't get what I want."

Say it again. "I DON'T NEED TO GET ANGRY JUST BEACUSE I DON'T GET WHAT I WANT."

That's how you forgive yourself for the past. You don't do it by saying, "Well hey, what I did was okay."

That's not how you bid the past adieu. You do it by saying, "What I'll do today will make a difference. It's now and the future that counts. Today is when the meter starts running. What was cannot be changed. What is and what will be depends on what I do today."

Why Mistakes are Okay

It's not that sex was the ultimate. It wasn't, it was higher—it was god. When you obtained it anyway you could, your world felt perfect. Intercourse—that's one way. Anal sex between guys—all the better. Oral sex between woman—sure. Masturbation—fine. Anything goes. You're flexible. What's that ridiculous saying, "Six of one or half a dozen of the other?" Give you the orgasm and leave you alone. That's how you feel about it. If you're horny, you want relief. How you get it really doesn't matter.

Oh sure, you began a relationship saying it mattered. You filled their ears with love-statements and promised them the world.

Liar! All you wanted was sex.

You had one empty relationship after another. After a while the scheme was predictable. Find a partner, romantically seduce them, superficially adore them, and score-big. If you didn't score big, lose them. Countless sexual encounters all followed this sequence.

A different scenario occurs if you're a loner. You've become a pro masturbator. Secretly, you've built a portfolio of erotic figures in your mind. They do what you tell them to do. They act as you command them to act. You are their king. They are your slaves, and the script never changes. Whether you hurt others, get hurt yourself, show love or receive love—you're still the captain. Steer your fantasies any way you like. It's your voyage. Nobody else is onboard.

When you reach the sensual height of orgasm, you've found nirvana. A state of perfect balance exists. You feel one with the world around you. Somehow, some way, you're completely happy. Nothing bothers you at this moment. You coast in a sea of pure serenity, unencumbered by any disturbing thoughts. Your mind goes into a trance. You zero in on deeply, soothing pleasure felt throughout your body. You melt as your muscles relax from a workout of seismic proportions. You're floating through mental space. It's ecstasy and you love every moment of it.

It doesn't last. Further, the more you do it, the shorter this blissful moment lasts. That's what is so imperfect about it—it doesn't endure. Here now, gone a moment later. Nothing you can do will bring your perfect sensation back immediately. Once the feeling of bliss is gone, you get hornier faster, so you naturally want sex faster.

Forget it, it doesn't happen that way. Things take time and people take time. You and somebody else are not machines. You can't push a button like the one on a pop machine each time you're thirsty for more sex. No matter how fast you want sex so you keep your high sensations, that high will drop. It won't drop slowly, but as fast and furiously as a brick falling from the Empire State building. When it lands, watch out. Crash! Emotions frazzle. You hate everybody and everything and every day is PMS. That is, until you have sex again.

One day you realize sex is fallible. It is imperfect and involves lots of mistakes. To help you see what I mean, complete the following statements:

1. I hate it when sex is over because I feel_____

_____

2. I hate it when sex is over because the other person always_____

_____

3. It never fails. Moments after an orgasm I am suddenly hit with__

_____

4. My climax has to be right or else I feel_____

Notice how quickly you had answers for these statements? You knew exactly how you thought. You always know how you think when it comes to imperfect sex. Ever realize that? Sex is never just all right. It's only okay, really wild this time, or maybe better than last time but is it superb? I'd say "no," probably never superb. Why is that?

Sex gets low grades for two reasons. First, you've done it so often you know what to expect. You attain a climax—whoopee. You want more so you try it again. Again, no thrills, just a repeater. It's okay, but you're competing for the gold. You push harder next time. Maybe you experiment with new ways or gamble with cutting off your oxygen, or inducing more stimulation by using drugs to reach a higher level of energy. Reach it and you're wired. Nearly reach it and you're upset.

A second reason sex is imperfect is *you. You make it imperfect.* You let so many things interfere with just purely enjoying the physical moment that all the fun goes away. Think of the things you do to fine-tune sex. Props, pictures, self-talk, talking to your partner, positioning—it becomes a game of *Twister*. It's confusing. You focus on all the gadgetry and mental rehearsals to achieve erotica, and what happens? Kaboom—something goes wrong. No, not your parts, they perform well.

Your outer body is doing what it's supposed to do. Inside is where the trouble lies. Your inner thoughts about making your experience perfect are obsessive. Thoughts keep coming. It's as if they have a mind of their own. You can't think of anything else. You hear echoes of the same questions whirling around your brain. Inside you hear yourself ask...

> *Did I look at the right pornographic picture?*
> *Did I say the right things to my partner?*
> *Did I do everything my partner wanted?*
> *Did I hit every step of erotica on target?*
> *What did I leave out?*

You desperately follow the ritual. Unfortunately, the more you feel sex is like a ritual of many steps all lined up in a perfect row, the more sex loses its spontaneity and fun. Lovemaking loses its romance. Orgasm loses its aphrodisiac effect. You get locked into being a robot who says and does exactly the same thing each time. No exceptions. No variations. Just do as the script says and don't change it.

Calibrated sex is a nuisance because it involves many parts. Never—absolutely never—do all of the parts of the ritual synchronize exactly as you say they should. It's Murphy's Law: *If something can go wrong, it does.* You've made sex too rigid, too methodical. You're calculating every movement to the second. Off a centimeter of a moment and you panic. Everything is ruined, sex dies. You are angry. Your partner is furious because you are so inflexible.

When sex is a strategic war of hit or miss—either you do it right or you do it wrong—guess what happens? You lose. You always lose. Sometimes, winners get a brief breeze of feeling great and think they can duplicate it every time. That's you. You're still stuck in the "I can do it, watch me!" stage of getting an erotic high. Every time you polish up the routine you insist your odds of achieving a perfect orgasm increase.

Go ahead, gamble with your sex life. See if you can beat the odds of earning a perfect sex score using all the vibrators, attachments and other paraphernalia. Maybe you will. Maybe this time you'll get lucky. Maybe you'll hit the jackpot twice in a row. You'll be a big shot in your mind—a person you perceive as confident, powerful, and sexually talented. You'll regard yourself as sensually irresistible and able to miraculously seduce any partner using your arsenal of tools and charm.

Sex won't be genuine. It will turn into a hunting match; you against them. You win. They lose. You'll prey on their innocence and feel important. You'll test out your killer instincts on an unsuspecting partner. You'll plug your victim into a preconceived formula. It will fit like a glove. In stages you'll lead them down the primrose path, knowing exactly what you're doing and how long it will take.

When it's over, you'll revel in victory. You'll gloat over seducing your partner in record time and perfecting the art of Don Juanism. Yes, you will have scored big again. This time maybe a home run. Face it, you're a mercenary for sex.

Why? To earn a gold medal? To feel certain you're the king or queen of lovemaking this side of the Mississippi? That's an honor, I suppose. On the other hand, perfecting sex in a methodical, unemotional, and fully selfish form has a dark side. It maintains your compulsive addiction for more sex for the wrong reasons.

Release your pressing urge to make sex better, best and perfect. Think of lovemaking like reading the paper. Sometimes you selectively sample important portions of the paper rather than consume every detail; sometimes you skim only the headlines. You read what you have time for. Sex can be a brief and simple experience as well with no pressure, no deadlines, and no unrealistic expectations. Perform it simply, skipping many parts of foreplay or, selectively sample the best parts of foreplay agreeable to you and your partner and immerse yourself blissfully. Sexual vitality is not how accurately the sequence, ritual, or steps flow together flawlessly. Real vitality comes from picking and choosing the best sequence or ritual of sex and letting things happen spontaneously.

Experience true unbridled passion without the annoyance of some scoreboard marking points for perfection. Begin to hear yourself review the following "I will" guidelines with your inner voice before you have sex:

1. *I will* do something different in foreplay.
2. *I will* ask my partner what he or she would like instead of the same-old routine.
3. *I will* stop somewhere between foreplay and intercourse and briefly state how much fun I'm having.
4. *I will* deliberately delay my preorgasmic needs until my partner is ready for me. I will prepare my partner first before I completely feed my needs.
5. *I will* laugh aloud about any mistakes I make. I also will respect mistakes my partner makes, whether that person laughs or ignores his or her mistake.
6. *I will* be playful, animated, and pay attention to my partner, making him or her feel I want them with me, instead of using them as a catalyst for my own pleasure.

Look Ahead Two Steps at a Time

Breaking the habitual chain of "I must make it perfect" is hard. You know the expectation of perfection is a pain in a neck. Every time you engage in petting or kissing or even talk about doing it, the same feeling comes over you, *"Will I do it right?"*

Right or wrong, sex has to be fun. That's the opposite of perfect. The demand for perfection robs natural romance of pleasure. Forget the savvy techniques and think less about your own orgasm to change the impulsive equation. Now you're not just having sex, you're being sexual—and being sexual is what romance is all about.

When you think of your body and your mind wants an orgasm, that's when it's time to switch from sex to romance. Do this by looking ahead two steps at a time. The two steps are always the same and you do them in order. One deals with delay; the other deals with being caring.

First the delay. Ask yourself, "What can I postpone or delay just for a minute or so?"

For example, you're starving for a kiss. You hope, of course, kissing will invite more sensual touching and that's why the kiss hits like a craving for sweets. Can you stop the overwhelming urge for kissing? Can you reroute the circuit of your libido, prevent your lips from puckering up and landing fully on your partner's mouth?

Yes, you can. Delay it. Stop yourself from imposing your need onto another person. Postpone it for one to five minutes. See what happens.

Delay is like saying, "No, I'm the president of my body and I just ordered myself to do something—no kissing! Not now, not yet. Wait. Wait patiently."

Stretch out time and space for a bit. You usually move at a rapid pace and don't dilly dally when you're driven. Except now. Now you will take a physical timeout. Sit in the chair in front of the television and start flicking the channels until something decent is on. Sit there vegetating for several minutes while you delay your need for kissing.

Go ahead and do it now, if you want to. Just put this book down for a second and stare at the television. Wait one to two minutes and then return to reading.

It wasn't that bad, was it?

When you can delay things, the second step is even simpler. It involves doing for others—your partner, to be exact. At the exact moment you're sexually active mind is conjuring up self-absorbing fantasy, that's when you switch gears. Think not of what you would enjoy; think of what your partner wants.

Hard, right? In fact, as you read that last sentence you really got turned off, didn't you? You're thinking, if I show that much caring to another person I'll be sucking up to them...and I'm no brown-noser.

Acts of sweetness seem like a bitter pill to swallow. Want to know why? I'll tell you. It didn't pay in the past to do kind things for people since nobody did anything good to you. Besides, if you start getting all pleasing and "lovey-dovey," it's inevitable your partner will expect you to keep it up. It would mean showing more affection, more attention to them, and less pleasure for you. Who would want to do that?

You would. You're not playing baby-sitter to a partner if you're pleasant to him or her. You're also not sucking up to them, or leading them to feel they can dominate you. You're not surrendering your identity or losing control. You won't get swallowed up by a whale.

Polite, caring behavior will not make you feel like you're purging your personality and pretending to be somebody else, but it will feel strange. You won't feel like *you* and this odd sensation may ruin your efforts.

Sherry thought that. She honestly believed that tenderness and polite remarks were ditzy. She figured she'd done her job; no more was necessary. She gave her partner oral sex; had intercourse with him at least once nightly, and let him touch her genitals whenever he wanted whether in private or in public. Sherry got off on this and knew her partner felt the same.

So, why do more? Why spoil a good thing? That was Sherry's thinking but she was a good sport and tried anyway. First she delayed her penetrating drive for sex. By the end of the first day she felt her insides boiling and her hunger for sex was insatiable. Nevertheless, she still abstained.

Then, she began being good to her partner, Fred. She smiled and talked with him an hour before they had sex. Usually, they never talk: they just fornicate. Not tonight. Sherry spent time and energy sharing personal bio-information and patiently listening to Fred talk about his day. She asked him questions about his feelings and waited for his answer. She looked directly into his eyes with undivided attention. All this was her contribution to "caring."

The verdict? She won. Fred was ecstatic. He felt so genuinely loved and overwhelmed by her attention he wanted to see her more, not just for sex, for dating. A month later, Sherry was embarrassed to admit what she had discovered. She found out how much fun she and Fred could have without their bodies on top of each other. She found simple pleasure in going to a movie, eating meals together, and just relaxing.

Well, if it's so good for Sherry; it can be good for you, too. The two steps to think about ahead of time go like this:
➢ First, delay your urge.
➢ Second, do something pleasant for your partner.

Pride has a new Face

Identity. How do you think of yourself—big, strong, athletic, attractive? Maybe you even think of yourself as irresistible? Your perception of you is a composite of many things. What people say to you is one. What you overhear people saying about you, that's two. Or, what you've come to think of yourself over many years. Good or bad, opinions form your identity. When you feel your identity has good qualities, those qualities give you a feeling of esteem or *pride*.

However, you have to be careful about what you call pride. For some, pride is money. How much they earn or spend is a measure of their personal worth. For them, pride consists of dollar signs. For others, pride is their weight. They are what the scale says they are. Heavy people suffer low pride and slender people gallantly feel high pride. Pride can be anything you choose—including your obsession for sex.

Deeply consuming thoughts about your next orgasm or who you'll do it with can be a matter of pride. Annette sincerely bought into this. She accepted the idea that her finest gift in life was her unbelievable lovemaking. Every guy she was with attested to it. No question about it, one thing Annette could do right was foreplay and intercourse. It was intoxicating.

Knowing this, Annette naturally felt proud of her incomparable achievement and felt any relationship could work if she had one opportunity to display her talents. Sexual pride overcame many fluctuations in relationships and averted several "almost-abuse" situations. She would release her aphrodisiac and enjoy the predictable outcome of charming her partner into submission. It was magic. Annette knew what strings to pull and when to pull them and she had no doubt in her mind she was doing the right thing.

Sex was who she was. Her pride stood for Sex Goddess. Then came the one problem—a guy who didn't like sex. She somehow stumbled into a relationship where, after a date or two, her lover-to-be refused her sensual overtures. He politely abstained. Call him Victorian, but it was true. He wanted something different from her—not a blow-job; not anal sex or some unusual position that challenged her sexual creativity. He demanded more than just the old tricks of her trade. She had to show another side of herself—a personal side filled with emotions, ideas and possibly even humor.

Freaked out, Annette had no idea what she could do. In fact, she desperately wanted to end the relationship but this guy was persistent. He would call her, invite her to breakfast, and even make dinner for her. Annette felt this was bizarre and did not know how to respond to his kindness. She dug deeply into her mind to figure out some strategy, some solution on how to react. None emerged.

She frantically realized she had to do something. So, she did. She broke up with him. After all, this guy "Doesn't like me for whom I am." Annette told herself he wanted somebody else, not me. He wanted someone I couldn't be. She convinced herself he was delusional. He wanted her in a way totally uncomfortable for her—he wanted her without sex. Annette couldn't hack it. She couldn't see the danger. Her *pride was blind. It prevented her from enjoying a healthy relationship.*

Annette's story is not unusual. Falling into this trap is easy. Sex becomes totally consuming, you live and breathe it. You act on physical and emotional sensations governed by impulses. The more you have sex, the more you like it. You become one with sex and your identity follows suit.

Annette, and many other people mistakenly confine their strengths to sex. Nothing else matters. Inside the boundary of sexual thoughts and activities lies a confident, proud YOU who responsibly can outperform, outshine, and out endure any person. You consistently rise above your own self-doubts, displaying pride in your masterful talents. You are proud of being sexual and know it works for you.

The danger of sex-pride is in its broad limitations—it simply doesn't work in 90% of your life. The 90% of life in which you have to talk, listen, negotiate, confront, get angry, be sad, and adapt. That's right, *adapt*. You can't adapt effectively if your only emotional equipment for adapting is sex. You can't grow as a person if all you feel you can do to fix things is having an orgasm. That is not solving problems, it's avoiding problems.

Say goodbye to sex-pride. So sad, too bad, and hate to see you go…

The real test of change is in your pride. It doesn't happen overnight, or in a month. However, shortly after, it does. Pride shifts as you shift from being a one-dimensional to a multidimensional person. When you start to see the world outside your bedroom, your pride sees it too. You become what you see and what you do.

Just Do, Don't Say You'll Do

The hardest part of changing your pride has nothing to do with changing your pride. In fact you may find changing easy. As with anything you say you'll do. "Oh, you'll see, I'll do it. No big deal, it will be a snap." As you say it, you really mean it. You don't doubt it.

Today, you're pumped with energy. You have high-charged voltage inside you electrifying your thought and really motivating you to change your habits. You can hear it echoing loudly inside, "I'm serious, today I'm really going to quit sex."

It is just like quitting smoking, not drinking coffee, not swearing, and not yelling at the kids. While we're at it, let's add not procrastinating. Did I miss anything?

New Year's resolution-fever. It happens when you suddenly realize you've really screwed up your life and you think the only way out is to promise yourself you'll never do anything bad again.

Really, swear to God, I won't do it again.

You do it again. Two days later the same old habits resurface. Those nasty rituals of talking, thinking and wanting sex arise in your mind urging you to be who you have been. Nothing different— back to the status quo. You feel normal—different behavior feels weird.

When you make hollow promises, you feel hollow. Inside you feel empty and unworthy. You figure you can't pull off a miracle of personality change so, hey, why bother? You conclude your habits are deeply rooted in rotten pathological illness and it would be too hideous to dredge up its roots and cut them off. Forget it—you're doomed. You sadly decide you're helplessly stuck in the mud of sexual obsession forever. You have no energy, no ambition and not a morsel of hope. Your situation is abysmal; let sleeping dogs lie.

Okay, you've rationalized your unfulfilled promises. You blame your failure on life's misfortunes. The more promises you break, the more life sucks, but that doesn't stop you or your life. You move on to meet new challenges.

You can coast through life like a feather and land wherever the wind blows you. Still, I don't think that's you. You don't operate that way. You want to know where you are going—you want to be in control.

No, you're not a feather; you're the wind. You can make things move in any direction if you first commit yourself to realistic change.

So for starters, don't promise anything—you can't keep promises. Think of new things. Trying different ways of doing things is like experimenting with new sexual positions. They may warrant a try but once you do, you're not committed to doing them forever—once may be enough.

Breaking the sex maniac record in your life is a matter of just doing. Try anything once; try it again if it feels okay. Try it a third time for kicks—and even a fourth if you think you're onto something. Regardless, don't promise you'll do it. Don't sing praises about what you're trying to do or what you'll gain from doing it. That sounds like a delightful sales pitch, but a lousy personal effort. Remember, if you're good at sex, you're good at talking sex.

When it comes to change—real change—talk is as bad as obsessing about sex. Talk to yourself, not about what you'll do and how you'll do it tomorrow. Instead tell yourself what change you can make today—this moment. For example, when you finish this chapter, don't masturbate, don't rendezvous with your partner, don't turn on a pornographic movie—delay it while you do something kind for somebody else.

That's doing, not *talking about doing*.

Real change begins with real behavior. As you try new skills in this and subsequent chapters, observe in yourself how well you do them. Don't patronize me or yourself by saying, "You'll see, I can do it."

You don't have to hear that pledge of allegiance. Forget it. Skip the "What I can do," stage and boldly try out one or two of the new behaviors you're reading about. When you do them and see yourself doing them, then you can say, "You see, I did it."

Do you know something? You really did do it.

Chapter Two
Why Bad Habits Linger

Betty insisted it would never happen again. She promised herself. Not a New Years resolution, not a "Yeah, right. I'll do it tomorrow" kind of thing. This time is for keeps—a commitment for life. She would never fall for the same type of guy again.

Which type? You know. The one who deeply satisfies her sexual needs. A month into her relationship with Brad she figured it out. "I get hot around him. He turns me on. I am talking power-orgasm here." Brad's sensuous magic was hard to refuse and Betty fell, hook, line and sinker. She bit the bait, *and she knew it*.

The magnetic hook didn't connect until the first time they made love. After that, breaking the spell was hard.

"I don't know how to describe it," she would say. "He could just touch me and I'd light up like a fire and orgasm in seconds. With my other boyfriends it would take hours for me to climax." Not with Brad. Brad's sexual power lured Betty into a seductive trap. She realized his personality was brash, cold, brutal and controlling. She tolerated his vulgarities and played along with his overimaginative sexual fantasies. She even overlooked being called "fat," "pig" and "bitch," just so she'd get stimulated by his fiery sexuality.

For Betty, craving Brad was compulsive—until she had enough. Not because sex died out, she could go on forever in that respect. Something else stopped her. Not always, but it did stop her often enough so that she began to rethink the relationship.

Betty thought about her dignity—what little she had left of it. She searched deeply into her heart for the strength to push aside her sexual cravings and stop the addictive cycle of being with Brad.

She had to do it. She no longer wanted the relationship, no longer wanted to be treated badly. She finally faced an ugly truth—sex isn't everything.

Betty's unrelenting habits are proof that sex is a powerful motivator and can perpetuate addictive cycles even when you want to stop the cycle. Think of Betty. For her, sex was everything but she finally stopped it from ruining her life. She suffered emotional disgrace and humiliation until she finally figured out it was time to stop. She stopped when destructive habits interfered to an intolerable level with her life.

This chapter tells you how to break the habit cycle *before* you hit bottom. It explains why habits linger and what you can do to catch yourself so you're not blindly flying on auto-pilot. You'll see how you unknowingly maintain habits you want to change. Why, even when you say you'll change, your habits win out.

Feels Right

Normal is just doing what comes naturally. Right? Think about it. You reply with "Thank you" when somebody compliments you because it sounds normal. You lie down in bed when you're tired because it feels normal. You do many other everyday things without thinking about them—wash your face, brush your teeth, eat meals, drink coffee, smoke cigarettes or chew gum—the list is endless. These and other personal habits are built on repetition. You repeat the activity day in and day out. Every day is the same. The habit feels right because your body is used to doing it. The habit itself isn't morally or legally right or wrong, just a regular part of your day.

For example, men awake in the morning with an erection because of the need to urinate and testosterone build up. They may ask their partner for sexual relief before getting out of bed and before going to the bathroom to relieve the erection. First it starts as a once-in-a-while thing. It feels so good the male partner is eager for a repeat performance the next morning. After two weeks of orgasm upon awakening, he now finds he cannot start the day without that orgasm. *It feels normal. It feels natural.*

Physically he is a changed person—he wants that stimulation. Before the habit began, his penis had the erection. Nevertheless, it was moderately firm and would weaken once he got out of bed. Now, the story is different. He wakes up with a far stronger erection. Immediately, he feels vital stimulation rushing through his penis in anticipation of sexual relief. If relief is by intercourse, he may advance to an intimate position even before his partner is ready—or awake! He begins his penetration as his arousal threshold is reached. It takes more stimulation to get that great feeling so he maintains a longer erection. Sex lasts longer, too.

He can't wait for his partner to help. If she's ready and willing, great. If not, he'll either pursue intercourse without her consent or masturbate himself while she is sleeping. One way or another, he believes he must do what feels normal.

Normal as it seems, this is not usual. Habits grow from strange and unusual beginnings. When something atypical happens, then happens again several times, the oddity vanishes. Now the unusual is replaced with normalcy.

Making love when you have company in the house is an example. Suppose you and your partner warmly snuggle up together after a long day of hosting guests staying at your house. One thing lead to another and the snuggling turns hot and passionate. Before you know it, the two of you are muffling your voices in a pillow while climaxing.

It feels great. Knowing people are in the bedroom upstairs is hilarious. The first time.

And the second time.

Even better the third time.

By the fourth time, sex is an electrical power plant energized by having people in your house. When you have friends sleep over, you can't wait to consummate your relationship.

Sex when visitors are in the house has become a habit. It feels normal. It may even replace previously, more traditional sex habits you and your partner shared. Now—you may find it strange to admit—you can only reach an orgasm when you have house guests. Other than with visitors, you and your partner feel frigid.

Normal it is not. It's an exception turning into the rule. It's a one-time experience becoming a routine. You know when it happens. You can feel it. You can even talk intellectually about it. You discuss it with your partner and decide you and he or she really should return to *normal* sexual behavior.

In practice, forget it. You can't return to previously normal sexual practices because now this new behavior has become the *normal* sexual practice.

Others Say It's Right

If you're doubtful about your habit, ask a friend for advice.

"Oh, sure, I'd do that too," you hear.

Now, don't you feel reassured?

You now have proof by consensus. If two people say it's normal, by God, it's normal. Make the count three, maybe even four people attesting your sexual habits are normal. Watch how your anxiety is relieved.

"Oh, thank God. I'm not crazy," you declare.

You're right. You're not crazy. You're in a bubble. Everyone you consulted lives in that bubble and sees the world as you see it. They all share your sexual cravings and sexual perspectives. You all operate on the belief that sex is a personal and biological expression. When you ask your sister if she gets it on with her husband three time a day and she affirms, "Of course, don't you?"

You quickly reply, "Certainly I do."

You're either lying or sexually thriving at a pace that fulfills a standard set by other people you trust and believe in—your parents, siblings, best friend. Maybe even those in authority such as college instructors and bosses. You may discover how seriously you take their opinions on sex.

For example, Hannah confided to her female boss in a weak moment that she and her boyfriend reciprocally performed oral sex in the "69" position. She elaborated how sensually absorbed she feels and now looks forward to sex this way every night. Hannah believes this represents the national average. She coerces her boyfriend into a nightly ritual of oral sex. She feels doing it that often is normal. He agrees and she loves it. "Just like my boss said I would."

The boss's approval made a habit feel valid. She gave credibility to an excessive ritual. The ritualistic aspect of their sexual habit doesn't phase Hannah and her boyfriend, though. They *seem* content. Of course, they can't fall asleep at night until each receives oral climax. Did I mention—neither person can reach climax any other way except through oral sex?

When Hannah's boss said their habit was good, it became gospel to her.

Scared to Change

The hardest pill to swallow is change. Nobody, I mean nobody, really likes change. Don't be fooled by zealous self-improvement gurus declaring in energetic pitches, "Anybody can change anything—look at me!"

While you're looking at his or her $700 suit and 6-digit sports car, you might buy into the fantasy. "I'd love to have those things. All I need to do is change," you say.

You may watch an infomercial selling motivational products. They are notorious for pushing the "You-can-do-it-too" miracle cure. They provide testimonials from satisfied customers who are fanatical about the product and are willing to say they owe their lives to the product.

I consulted on infomericals as scriptwriter and expert and would deliberately use language that "sold" the product. Products marketed successfully were those that grabbed the impulse-buying customer in seconds. The customers who delayed and smart shopping customers ignored the products.

Sales are built on a philosophy that change is a mental state and can be turned on and off at the snap of your finger.

Change does not happen that way—at least not with sex. Sex is a habit you don't want to change—at least at first. The reason is clear. It is FEAR.

Take a moment and answer the following questions with a YES or NO:

1. If I stop performing sex the way I like it, I'll feel deprived, cheate, and miserable. ☐YES ☐NO
2. If I stop performing sex the way I like it, I'll get angry and irritable. My partner and I will not get along. ☐YES ☐NO
3. If I stop performing sex the way I like it, I'll forget how to have sex and won't like it any other way. ☐YES ☐NO
4. If I stop performing sex the way I like it, I'll lose interest in my partner and we'll probably break up. ☐YES ☐NO
5. If I stop performing sex the way I like it, I'll start bingeing on food, alcohol or develop some other habits to make up for not enjoying sex. ☐YES ☐NO

Count your answers. Did you answer five (5) as YES? 100%? Give yourself an "A" for "Anxiety."

Your score is perfect because stopping sex the way you like it means stopping something very near and dear to you—orgasm. You like it and you want it. Not much in the world outside erotica turns you on. In addition, you experience anxiety when you think about not feeling good. All the fears associated with no sex—or no sex the way you like it—are too painful to bear. You would feel what you don't want to feel. You would feel vulnerable and out of control.

Honestly saying, "Yes, I can do it; I can lower my sexual appetite" means coming face to face with ugly, anxious fears about your life. It pits you against your inner enemy—self-love. You're already a prisoner of self-love and presuming there is no escape from it. You feel trapped in a vicious, no-way-out circle. An area where everything you do feels right but is wrong and things you do right (not having sex) feel wrong but are right. It seems futile.

You have entered the **SEX-EQUALIZER ZONE**. It is located:

➢ In the middle of wanting to do something and not knowing how to do it.
➢ Right after you feel anxious and aren't sure how to relieve the anxiety.
➢ Just before you give up and say "It's not worth the struggle."

Yes, it is worth it.

For now, while you are in the SEX-EQUALIZER ZONE you don't have to commit to a decision. You face many possible options—to have sex, not to have sex, have sex this way, that way, or a totally different way. The ZONE is like a weigh station—something like purgatory. You'll stay there until you figure out where you *want* to be. Your lifestyle stays about the same and sex habits are ongoing. However, your mind is not resting. Night and day you are ruminating about what you should do. The SEX-EQUALIZER ZONE is not a fun place. You are there because of indecision. You won't exit it until you make a decision.

Five simple rules can get you out of this limbo. They're easy to do and fast to learn. Read each of the rules aloud and picture yourself doing them.

SEX-EQUALIZER ZONE RULES:

1. *I will look at sex as if it is an inanimate object.* I will picture it as something I can see, touch, take or let go. I can walk away from it and it will not hurt me.
2. *I will look at orgasm as a personal choice.* I can make it happen or prevent it. I, and I alone can tell my body when I want an orgasm and when orgasm is unnecessary. I firmly take control over this decision—nothing can force me to choose against my will.
3. *I will look at partners as people, not as objects.* The opposite of number one. Sexual partners are living, emotional beings who hurt when I use them. They are not toys, games or unfeeling objects. They cannot be shaped, molded, manipulated and tossed away after I use them. They are not disposables. I will look at their inner personality and spend more time caressing their feelings than caressing their outer body. I will show them love inside before I show them love outside.
4. *I will look at my body as one among many parts of me that make me feel secure.* Physical exterior is not the only gauge of my dignity and emotional stability. I have a smart brain and sensitive feelings. These are not handicaps. They work in a tandem with my physical body to present me as a singular person. This total person represents who I am and what I can do in life. Shaping my body or tuning up my mind only won't carry the weight. All of me adds up to compile the complete picture of what I have to offer people.
5. *I will stimulate all parts of my person, not just my body.* All of me constitutes my esteem. I can trigger excitement in any part of my personality, from the tips of my thoughts to the bottom of my emotions. My body does not have one receptor—my genitals.

Inside my body lie thoughts, opinions, and passion—all running on empty. I can electrify them in many ways. My exterior also has many other stimulating avenues, not just carnal arousal.

Aerobics, sports, playing a musical an instrument are some of the infinite ways for me to vibrate parts of my body other than my sex organs.

SEX-EQUALIZER ZONE RULES are for your protection. They keep you from falling off the wagon. They hold you together like a strong adhesive when you want to pull apart or slip into old habits. They raise your confidence to a level you can believe in. Yes, sex-equalizer rules are your personal compasses through a densely thick forest. You may not know in which direction to go but you know what to expect when you get out. You get *you* back. You'll feel alive, really in control. It will be as if you've taken a long bath. Cleansed and free, you'll be a new person able to start over in a sexual world where your mind and body are not slaves to orgasm.

Stupid is What Stupid Feels

The first baby-steps you take out of the SEX-EQUALIZER ZONE are slow, clumsy and humiliating. You know you'll feel stupid. After all, when was the last time you started your day not thinking about sex? Like, never?

Now you do. You awake in a world where thoughts are about other things, not just sex. Where you begin your day as most people do, focused on a job, family, or plans for the evening. Your ears plug into the morning news as your mind soaks it up. Thoughts fade in and out about household and personal expenses, about food you'll eat for lunch and dinner, and about friends you'll call.

On average, your inner ear will listen to conversations you tell yourself several times a day, sometimes repeating the same message, other times in a creative, problem-solving way. Inner-ear conversations occur when you talk to yourself about life's ups and downs and how to resolve them.

Sure, you do that now but much of your self-talk is filled with smut. Try it without the barrage of sexual thinking. Try it without saying to yourself how beautiful that girl is, or how absolutely gorgeous that guy is. Ignore the flood of ideas on how to lay this or that person.

Think of your mind as an empty field. You can choose to plant whatever you want in it. Either you can treat it like a dump sight and fill it with sexual talk or you can keep the erotica out of it. Save your empty field for a luscious garden. Plant it with seeds of real life issues where you can reflect on your personal happiness growing from things other than sex. For example, remember how pleased you were when you got a promotion; how pleased your neighbor was when you did a kind thing for her. These are life's simple pleasures out of which your seeds can grow and blossom into loveliness.

Self-talk turns healthy when you make the switch. Of course, not at once because nothing usually happens that way. At first the deliberate shifting of sexual thoughts to nonsexual thoughts feels odd. You're not used to interrupting your thoughts. You've just gone along with whatever entered your mind—most of it perverted.

Your thoughts are shifted away from lust but you can't expect your perverted thoughts to simply go away. They still happen and part of you is pushing to listen to them. The more you insist, "No, I won't listen to sex-thoughts," the more they become like a force out of control. The perverted thoughts launch an attack upon your psyche so vicious you're bound to do battle with them.

You'll feel absolutely retarded when you push yourself to be a nonsex thinker while parts of your mind force sex-thoughts back in. It's a tug-a-war and you are not used to it. Part of your mind will say, "I don't get it, why not just do what feels naturally and be done with this struggle."

I'll tell you why you can't do that.

Because stupid is what stupid feels. If you feel dumb, you'll think you're dumb for thinking nonsexual thoughts You'll hop back to sexual thoughts where you feel smart and in control. That's not really a solution. You may think you have eliminated feeling stupid and everything is okay. You'll feel better—for a while. You may even say, "See, I told you I couldn't do it."

You're right in a way. You can't change without feeling stupid. Stupidity is a must. However, feeling stupid doesn't mean you are stupid. It means you're onto something new and exciting. It signifies you've finally taken the big plunge out of the safe zone and into the SEX-EQUALIZER ZONE.

You see, you have to feel stupid to be a different person. Stupid is exactly the right feeling during the metamorphosis from sex maniac to nonsex maniac. You can only walk across the bridge to freedom after you suffer periods of thinking, "Is this for real?"

Maybe you even dump on yourself, saying, "This is a farce. I feel like an actor and I don't think this is natural."

Darn right you don't. Don't expect miracles. You'll feel weird for a while. You'll even doubt your efforts are working since every other thought in your mind is stupid, stupid, stupid.

Good, that means you're doing it right.

Good, that means you're really working the system.

Finally, good, that means you're really changing.

I "Gotta" Do It

You're off to a good start. You are aware your new thoughts will feel awkward and you feel okay about that. Of course, be prepared for feeling like you're forcing it. The more you push and it feels fake, the better your progress—quantum leaps of progress.

Then suddenly, you'll be struck with an idea. "Cool, I can do this stuff—no problem."

Confident and filled with energy, you set your sights higher, thinking you can plow through any obstacle. "Hey, I got this far, I can go the rest of the way."

Beware of overconfidence. Confidence is good; feeling high and almighty is not good. That's when you do a nose-dive and spiral downward back to Earth. You don't want that, you want a compromise. You want ambition and enough energy to pull you out of the trenches, but make your ascending climb flexible. Do what you know you can do, but do it at a realistic pace.

Plan for obstacles. Say right off the bat, "I'm fallible, I make mistakes."

It's a good thing you're mortal. Mortals are imperfect. The gauge to measure how good or bad you're doing is, "How many mistakes do I make?"

Fred wouldn't see it that way. He believed you get better when you make no mistakes. "Perfecto-thinking," he called it. Put yourself in a mind-set of doing things right, then everything falls into place. Fred insisted this was a fact. He would go to work pumped up like an inflated balloon, sure he would be immune to errors. Sure, he would goof things up, but motivated as he was, trivial mistakes didn't phase him. He would laugh at the nonsense of errors and remind himself he was on a winning track.

Fred watched infomerical king, Tony Robbins's self-powering motivation. He saw how a positive mind can bolster confidence. Emulating Tony Robbins, Fred jumped on the "I-can-do-it-too" bandwagon and figured he could live a positive life.

Each time Fred felt sexual urges arising, he'd say to himself, "I'm positive, strong, and better than these urges."

Fred was his own cheerleader. He told himself he could lick anything because he wouldn't make mistakes. The less mistakes he made, the less chance that he'd fall off the wagon. Day in and day out he injected these high-charged words into his mind until he memorized the phrases by heart. Fred's goal was to be so solid internally that he could fight off external sexual urges.

Fred forgot something—*He's mortal*. He does make mistakes and he became so obsessed about not making mistakes that he thought about mistakes all the time. He would wake up hearing his inner voice cheer him on, a regular mental booster club. All day long he would ruminate, "I'm doing great—no mistakes; I'm doing great—no mistakes." Unfortunately, while pumping himself up about what he won't do, he actually made himself more aware of his mistakes and more afraid of making them.

Fred did what so many people do. They automatically think the less mistakes you make, the better you're doing. Sounds right, doesn't it? If you smoke fewer cigarettes, you're cutting down. If you drink less alcohol, you're becoming more sober. If you resist intercourse, you're in more control of your sexual habits.

Sure, but once you put these "Gotta-do-its" in the forefront of your mind as Fred did, something unexpected happens. For example, you have urges to have intercourse:

1. *If I don't keep thinking of sex, I won't want sex.* This really turns into a mess. You keep thinking about not thinking about sex. Your mind is constantly preoccupied with ways to ignore, overcome and forget wanting sex.
2. *If I fight off all my sexual urges, I won't want sex.* It sounds reasonable but wait until you try it. Insulating yourself from normal human drives is not only impossible, it makes you angry. The more you stop, push away or yell at yourself for having sexual urges, the more you feel you are being deprived of having your way.

The big mistake in pushing perfect abstinence from having sexual urges is that the more you won't tolerate making mistakes, the more you're consumed with the mistakes. Then, you get angry with yourself for thinking about mistakes.

A good friend of mine, Damon Reinbold, international hypnotist for smoking cessation, once said to me. "Doug, I don't teach smokers to stop smoking because then they'll still think of smoking. I teach smokers to be nonsmokers. Then, they'll think like nonsmokers."

Nonsmokers, like nonsex maniacs, think the same way. They never worry about persistent mistakes since they look at the world differently. They see the world as full of mistakes they are free to make. They realize they have the willpower to prevent or interrupt those mistakes once they occur.

Unlike Fred, don't allow the Tony Robbins philosophy of positive thinking and being mistake-free. Think like nonsex maniacs who encounter normal sexual urges every day. They experience them and navigate through their urges.

They don't sit around anticipating when the next urge will hit. They don't constantly plan ways to fight normal sexual urges. Nonsex maniacs do not say, "I gotta do it right." They wait until the urge hits, then allow their skills and talents to work for them. You are learning those skills and talents from this book.

Then What Happens?

After you agree you make mistakes and plenty of them, what's next? How about trusting yourself? Can you do that? That's a doozy, isn't it?

Trust is making a promise to yourself—you do what you say and you say what you do.

There are three ways to begin trusting yourself when handling sexual urges. First, promise a friend or significant other what you plan to do and when you'll do it. This can be about anything, not just sex.

Second, tell the significant person or friend what you plan to do about sex. Later, tell them how you followed through with your plan. Third, be your own friend. Tell yourself what you plan to do. Remind yourself when you did what you promised you'd do.

Let's go through these approaches again:

HOW TO BUILD TRUST IN YOURSELF:
1. Tell a friend or significant other what you plan to do.
   - ☐ Tell them exactly what you plan to do. It can be about abstaining from sex or some other activity unrelated to sex.
   - ☐ Tell them within the day how you followed through on your promise.
2. Tell a friend or significant other what you plan to do about sex.
   - ☐ Tell them exactly what you plan to do about no sex or something related to control over sexual urges.
   - ☐ Tell them within the day how you followed through on your promise.
   - ☐ Tell them the mistakes you made and how you corrected those mistakes.
3. Tell yourself what you plan to do and how you followed through with it.
   - ☐ Tell yourself exactly how you'll interrupt or prevent sexual cravings.
   - ☐ Remind yourself later that day what you did to follow through on your promise to yourself.
   - ☐ Remind yourself it's okay to make errors.
   - ☐ Focus on what you did to overcome the errors rather than what you did to prevent the errors.

The biggest headache in eliminating cravings is not the cravings, it's the pressure you put yourself under when you believe you can't make mistakes. Yes, you are head and shoulders above many people who are not reading this book and not trying. However, mistakes are normal and you must experience them, all of them, to beat these pesky habits.

Chapter Three
Defuse the Habits Now

She loved his hands. That's right, *his hands*. Sally couldn't explain why. She knew it seemed crazy but that's the way it was. She is not sure when this habit started but it was powerful. It would make or break a sexual relationship for her.

She would meet a guy for the first time. He would be sweet and toss out casual chitchat-free-spirited lines of, "So, what do you do for a living?" Sally, knowing this gig, would be polite. She would talk with many guys during the evening and would end up bored by their trivial conversation. Some of them were handsome, some not. Some were professionals, some not. It seemed like a blur.

One thing she always remembered about a man— his hands. Thin, clean hands would turn her on. Sally admitted a guy's hands were the gauges for deciding if she wanted to pursue him for dating and a sexual relationship. Other things counted, of course, such as, is he friendly, relatively competent, and funny. However, his hands better pass the test or forget it.

Her sexual cravings lit up like fireworks when a man's fingers were long and thin, his hands unblemished, and his nails manicured. A perfect hand meant a perfect gentlemen. She could forget about other behaviors if those hands earned an A+.

Sally's penchant for hands got her into some ugly predicaments. She fell for guys who would promise her the rainbow, but deliver, to put it mildly, much less than a rainbow. She would dive head first into a romance thinking this man was perfectly right for her. Months later, Sally's surprise was always the same when promises were never kept and lies built on lies slid trust down the tube. His silicon hands were as phony as his behavior.

Sally realized the only way for her to stop sexually trusting unworthy men was to change her criterion about hands. She did. She followed the blueprint for change discussed in this chapter. You can follow in Sally's footsteps by making each device feel like it's your own personal tool for change. You'll see, it's not as bad you think.

Five-step Way to Say "No."

You're now on "urge-patrol." Suit-up and get your weapons loaded. You'll be walking around your house and in public as if you're packed with ammunition for combating a powerful enemy force—your urges. Urges don't surrender easily. They're feisty characters. You've wanted some things badly so your mind and body have become tough and stubborn over the years. You don't want to give up your urges. Your mind and body are not too excited about changing either.

In spite of all that, you will change. You know you can't function with sexual cravings on the brain. You can't think straight, talk straight or live a normal, healthy life when you are consumed with orgasm-withdrawals. It is a fight to the finish, but you'll see. You *will* win.

You do need a good arsenal. Body-builders have one; Olympic divers have theirs; and dieters always have theirs. Their arsenal always includes *Stoppers*.

Stoppers are ways you can say "No!" "No" can feel like torture unless you make two promises to yourself from the beginning. One promise is you'll have setbacks and it is okay. Remember—to err is to be human.

Second, promise yourself you'll use *Stoppers* for yourself—not for somebody else. You may think you're doing someone a favor by not having sex —and maybe you are—but first and foremost is what you do for you. *Stoppers* are for your own agenda. You want to anticipate, interrupt or prevent habits before they overwhelm you.

So much for promises. Now, what is a *Stopper*? Consider the law of *Stoppers*:

Laws of Stoppers
1. Saying "No" when you want to say "Yes."
2. Saying "No"when somebody else wants you to say "Yes."
3. Saying "No"when you're afraid to say "No" and really don't want to say "Yes."
4. Saying "No" and meaning "No."

Each of the four laws sets your *Stoppers* in motion. First, saying "No" when you want to say "Yes" means you have internal conflict. You're fighting a raging battle of wits. The tug-a-war has impulsive pleasure on one side pulling the daylights out of your willpower on the other side.

Second, saying "No" when somebody else wants you to say "Yes" means you're okay with saying "No" but at what cost? Just thinking that your refusal to have sex will annoy another person may scare you. You may buckle under pressure and go against your better judgment.

Third, saying "No" when you're afraid to say "No" but don't want to say "Yes" means you're easily intimidated. The person you have the hots for is sucking you into his or her trap. You think your only way to feel good and feel esteemed is to get it on with this person. You're full of fear. Don't blow it now, you're thinking. One false move and it's over for good. You surrender, hoping you'll change your mind midway through.

Nice try. You don't change your mind after you give in.

Fourth, saying "No" and meaning "No" is worlds apart. You may have enough assertiveness to refuse sex or any type of erotica. Good job! However, do your words last only for the moment or perhaps the entire evening? Are you lying to yourself? The promises you make to yourself may vanish when you feel lust. Excited and wanting sex speak louder than the words "No, I won't do it."

With *Stoppers* so important, is there a handy way to use them that can guarantee you won't slip back into bad habits?

Yes, if you use the *Stoppers* correctly.

Five Step Way to Use Stoppers: Refuse, Remove, Revise, Reward, Recover

1. **Refuse.** Stand up on your own two feet and push the words "NO, I DON'T WANT YOU," out of your mouth. Give yourself an emotional spine. Fight inner fears that you may annoy the person. Fight thoughts of shame because you feel bad for disappointing another person. You may upset them, you may ruin his or her day but you must speak and think according to what you know is best for you. Someone may tell you being sexual is best for you. Don't believe it, choose for yourself.

2. **Remove.** After you refuse sex, don't stick around and don't be a martyr. You may not want to be a coward. You'll think running away is cheap, immature, and doesn't confront your enemy face to face. You are absolutely correct in many conflict situations, but this one is different. The longer you stay at the scene after saying "No," to sex, the higher the likelihood that your partner thinks you're changing your mind.

   Are you? Just in case you're losing willpower, get out immediately. Excuse yourself and leave so you don't have to struggle with pros and cons of satisfying erotic cravings. Once you say "No," don't vacillate—No is No.

3. **Revise** Once you're out of there, find something else to do. Doing nothing puts you on Death Row. You'll sit there stewing over your decision—was it wrong? You will fantasize about what it would have been like to have sex.

Instead, you must act fast. Start a new task or activity the opposite of what you have been doing. Revise the situation. Whatever you choose to do, it should be mutually incompatible with what you were doing. Meaning—choose an activity to do that cannot occur at the same time as what you were doing.

For example, it's late at night. You are watching TV with your boyfriend. He's sitting close and puts his arm around you. You encourage him to do so. He pulls you close to him, ready to give you a big smooch. No problem. It's okay at first. Now you're kissing fully on the mouth, and his arms are around you. You love the way tingling sensations rush through your body. You feel pulsations in your vagina. You're excited and sure you're sending him the message that you are turned on.

That's when you say, "Excuse me, let's do something else." You remove yourself from the situation and revise it by asking him to join you in the kitchen. You seat yourself across from him at the table. No way short of a miracle can he swallow your lips and reexcite you physically while he's sitting some feet away from you across the table. That's what "mutually incompatible" means.

4. **Reward.** Okay, you made it this far. Nevertheless, don't get too self-assured. It's not over yet. Hopefully, once you're out of a situation, your sex mood is gone—for the moment. Removing yourself and diverting to a new activity is a timeout. You get a brief relief from the undertow of sexual cravings. However, it's only a matter of time before the next wave of addictive impulses strike. You want a mechanism you can install now before the wave reappears and you're up and surfing again.

Reward yourself. Literally say aloud, "Isn't this enjoyable?" You praise yourself and the person you're with for doing something besides sex. If you're alone, give yourself a pat on the back. Self-praise is not a cheap trick—you really deserve applause. Lavish yourself with it. Tell yourself why your revised task or activity is wonderful and really makes you feel better.

Your goal is to think, "I am so happy I did something else," rather than "Gee, I almost didn't escape that trap." Focus on what you did right, not on what you *almost* did wrong.

5. **Recover**. Even after self-praise, erotic sensations may not go away. Picture this scenario if you can: Your girlfriend and you are playing cards after both consenting not to have sex. However, you're not concentrating on the card game. You don't know if you flipped an ace of spades or Queen of hearts—nor do you care. All you can think about is your penis throbbing and driving you crazy. Inner obsessions eat away at you—you must get relief. The inner debate gets louder, tougher to resist. You're close to giving in.

Nevertheless, you don't surrender. You hold strong for one last step in the *Stopper* plan—recovery. It's doing a quick emotional healing on your body and your mind. It's like mental therapy. You're the therapist and patient at the same time. You say to yourself how deeply this inner debate hurts you and that you wish it were over. You tell yourself how afraid you are that you might surrender and have to start over. You confess your lowest point of vulnerability; you say you're feeling helpless and know it's scary.

By openly expressing your inner pain, you have just released the drives underlying your sexual habits. Drives push you to the brink of carnal pleasure because you ride them like a roller coaster. Your moods go up and down without your thinking, "Why am I like this?" You are usually on auto-pilot, being pulled in many directions. You are like a floating feather.

Now you are different. Now you've unearthed the underlying emotional hurt and lifted it up to the surface of your consciousness. You can hear your thoughts loud and clear through the speakers of your mind. Auto-pilot is turned off. You're driving your body manually.

The self-therapy you go through is more than a pep talk. It stimulates your awareness of what you're doing and why you're doing it. When you tell it to a trusted friend or significant other—such as the person with you with whom you refused to have sex—you'll be in even better shape.

Three ways others can help you say "No."

Self-restraint is difficult. When you accomplish it, you're amazed. You say, "Did I do that?" You are surprised about how easy following all five steps of *Stoppers* was. Once you get into the steps, they flow naturally. It is similar to preparing food before you eat it—you just do it. It is a habit. You're in the captains chair calling the shots.

Trouble is, what you want may be different from what somebody else wants. Craig couldn't believe this. He was, in his opinion, "Mr. Stud." Nobody, he thought, matched his distinctively smooth style of seducing women into sex. Craig wasn't kidding himself. He was an expert—calm, calculated, and in control of his prey. Lovers he scored with all wanted long-term relationships with him. At first, Craig enjoyed the flood of flattery, but never seriously considered their proposals.

He tried living with a woman two years ago but the relationship soon went belly-up. He tried to love and saw it literally get liquidated before his eyes. He came home early one afternoon and discovered his partner romantically busy with another guy. So, after that experience, he decided to play the field a bit more.

Craig finally realized his barfly one-nighters were getting old. He put the *Stoppers* method to work and found it initially was a blocker. He could put the brakes on when he eyed a perfect candidate for his seduction. It was hard, but doable.

Craig couldn't explain what happened to him next. Instead of cruising and flirting with women, he just went to the bar to shoot pool with his male friends. After one week he was getting the strangest phone calls from platonic female friends who said, "I don't get it, Craig. Five young women called me last night and were upset at you for being rude. Like, what's your problem, Craig?"

Craig was speechless.

Well, good news. The women saw the new Craig, but Craig hadn't seen the new Craig. They were faced with a different, nonseductive, nonflirtatious guy doing his own thing—*and they didn't like it.* They wanted him the way they were used to him.

Being disliked for being different doesn't feel good to Craig. Trying to be a friend instead of a sexual predator didn't pay off. Strangely, his female friends wanted back his old smiley personality—his old habits of relating to them. The reason is simple: *People stick with their comfortable habits. They don't want to change just because you change.* Craig's discipline was a personal goal but it felt like a personal failure. His only way to turn this bad scene around was to help his friends say "No" with him.

Enlisting people to say "No" with you doesn't happen overnight and it's not as simple as waving a magic wand over their heads. Sorry, no simple solution, but it *can* happen. Here are three ways to do it.

1. Ask them to do something different with you.
2. Thank them for accepting your decision.
3. Offer them another reward.

First, remove yourself from trouble before you relapse into discarded habits. Ask the person who is upset with you to do something different with you. For example, next time Craig played pool at the bar, he asked some ladies if they'd like to watch and play pool. He's never shared this type of activity with women before this. He either held them hostage one-on-one at a secluded table while showering them with flattery or lured them into his clutches after a single at the bar counter. Playing pool socially was a big step.

Second, when they go along with your new activity, be courteous. Say "Thank you." Assertively state your appreciation because your friends chose to spend time with you.

Speaking out directly is different from sending messages by sexual nonverbal cues. When you use nonverbal language, you're hoping the other party gets the message. Maybe they do. In Craig's case, they did—loud and clear. However, the message they received was always sensual. They knew from his eye contact and gestures that he wanted to go to bed with them.

Now, Craig doesn't give those nonverbal cues. He states the message in no uncertain terms that he just wants to have fun. That's Craig's full message. His previous female "regulars" may still read into his remarks and persuade themselves he's really saying what he used to say—he wants them for sex. They are wrong—Craig says what he wants to say and it doesn't include sex.

When people accept your "Thank you for spending time with me," reward them for it. You can be loving, playful, and a social butterfly without sex. Craig, for example, treated a couple of women spectators to a beer but did not flirt with them like he used to.

In your case, compliment your significant other for respecting your decision not to have sex and to do something else. Spend time with your special person without sex. Treat him or her to a meal, entertainment or other event as proof that you're genuinely grateful for how they have responded.

Whoops! No Substitute Habits

Stoppers really do end sex drives. They pull the plug on your circuit breaker. You can't cheat when you're using *Stoppers*. If you do cheat, you're not using a *Stopper*.

Of course, there is a way to cheat while using *Stoppers* but it's not due to the *Stopper* itself. It's due to a loop hole—a glitz in the *Stopper* system that may be all the room you need to restart old habits. The glitz is using substitutes for your habits. You're not having sex or even doing anything that in the past led to sex so on the surface, everything looks cool.

Substitutes are tricky. They look, taste and smell as if everything is great. No slip-ups here, right?

Wrong.

When you think you're using a *Stopper* but you are feeling just as good as you did before using a *Stopper*, then you're not using a *Stopper*.

Feeling good and "normal" when first using a Stopper is a sign of old, comfortable habits.

Habits shift back into form when many substitutes replace the real habits for a short time. You can tell if what you're doing is a substitute:

A SUBSTITUTE IS WHEN...

1. You're doing everything exactly the same way you've always done it except you're not having sex.
2. You've said "No" to sexual intercourse but you're having verbal or physical foreplay.
3. You've said "No" to sex but you're doing things that always lead to sex.
4. You've said "No" to sex but you're with people who always get you to have sex.

First, change in one entity causes changes in other entities. For example, throw a rock in the middle of a pond. Notice when the rock strikes the water it makes a rippling effect. You see circles leading out to the middle of the pond. The ripples affect the entire pond, not just the spot where the rock hit the water.

Behavior is like that. Changes you make in one place ripple out in your life affecting other things you do and the people with whom you do them. This rule of life has no exceptions.

When you think you've made a dramatic change and are proud of it, test this rule of life. Are you different in many other situations? Do people react to you in a way they haven't in other situations? If they do, you win. If they don't, you lose and, not only do you lose, you also haven't changed.

Second, saying "No" is only half the battle. You have to put your money where your mouth is. In other word, your actions have to match your words. Saying, "I don't want sex" doesn't have any significance if you are naked with your partner and involved in heavy petting and kissing. It may feel great but you're not using any *Stoppers*. Sensual touching is having sex—just as much as having sexual intercourse is. You may not think so, but it is. Foreplay heightens your arousal into a state of mind where your thoughts turn erotic and, physically, you become highly excited. That's about as close to coitus as you can get without intromission.

Third, you think you're on top of the first two substitutes. You've made substantial changes in your life and you're not teasing yourself by being sexually stimulated. What about getting high? What if sex is routine when you've drank five to seven beers, or smoked marijuana? If you use cocaine, peak arousal may put you in a state where all you can think about is sexual relief.

Drugs are bad and it is well-known you should quit them, but be practical. Drugs you used to stimulate excitement and often leading to intercourse are just like foreplay. They are substitutes for habits you're trying to abolish.

Drugs are one among many types of cues. Cues trigger your desire for sex and put you in a ready-state-of-mind for getting an orgasm. You may find places you go are cues for sex—a bar, a drive in your car, seeing certain movies and even visiting relatives. Craig, for instance, toyed with his habits by returning to the bar. However, he made so many changes in what he did while he was there that it helped him to stay focused.

Fourth, self-discipline can go to pot when you're always with a person who wants sex. Strong as you are, you can lose your willpower around this person's sensual personality. Statements he or she makes, things they do and the suave routine to which you've grown accustomed quickly makes you vulnerable. Targets of sex are cues. You want to spot them, deal with them and apply all five steps of *Stoppers* when around them.

Never assume your confidence is so great that you can ignore cues.

Good Things to Do Instead

The redeeming quality of using *Stoppers* and keeping both eyes out for substitutes is what it does for you. You feel ten feet tall. You can't believe the enormous lift of confidence you experience when you're in a world where everything makes sense. What you accomplish is due to your own efforts.

Using *Stoppers* is a fast method of breaking cravings before they devour your mind and body. With them, you can change yourself, change the way others respond to you and become acutely aware of your right and wrong actions.

You are your own monitor but don't take my word for it. Here are some really nifty ways to prove you're scoring big points. Assess your progress by answering "yes" or "no" to the following questions:

1. Are you thinking about your private parts all of the time?
 ☐YES ☐ NO
2. Are you doing everything the way you used to?
 ☐YES ☐ NO
3. Do you still see people or go to places to have sex?
 ☐YES ☐ NO
4. Do you have difficulty refusing sex or orgasm?
 ☐ YES ☐ NO
5. Do you do lots of other things to pamper your body?
 ☐YES ☐ NO
6. Do you deeply miss daily orgasm or doing things sexually?
 ☐YES ☐ NO
7. Do you give in to people wanting sex?
 ☐YES ☐ NO

8. Do you feel you have to be perfect to fight your habit?
   □ YES □ NO

This quickie checklist is your personal thermostat. You want a cold reading? You are healthy and doing well if you can answer all the questions as "NO."

If you answer some questions with "YES," it means you're still in the trenches. It means you've pulled up your sleeves and are ready to fight but scared to throw the first punch. The best cure for fear is curiosity. Be curious about what it would feel like to not have sexual cravings.

The idea mentioned earlier of being a nonsex maniac is why you should be curious. When you are a nonsex maniac, you don't worry about wanting sex. It doesn't cross your mind. Sure, affection is desired but not passion. Not always, not every minute of every day of every hour. You can concentrate better when you are not scheming what you'll do later or whom you will do it with.

Obsessive sexual fantasies never arise since your thoughts are on simpler and routine things. Nonsex maniacs look at more in the world than achieving sensual relief.

Your mind shifts gears to a healthy balance of affection. You see it for what it really is, not what you expect it to be. You'll be tuned into the right mental station, not the porno-station and not the Christian Broadcast Network. Love takes on an entirely new meaning. Here is how you will see love:

1. You'll see people as people, not as objects.
2. You'll see love as caring, not as making love.
3. You'll see sex as compassion, not as climax.
4. You'll see yourself as flexible, not as rigid.
5. You'll see your partner as a friend, not as a playmate.

Powerful sexual cravings vanish when you stop thinking like a sex maniac. Now, let's keep up the momentum and really put the squeeze on your sex habits.

Chapter Four
Tempted to Give Up?

Elizabeth swore she made a mistake. "No way," she insisted, "I never thought this would be so hard." No, she wasn't celibate. Liz couldn't pull that off if you paid her. She loved sex too much—and knew it devoured her. However, she did what these chapters have asked her to do—have sex in moderation.

She said, "Fine, I'll give it a whirl." She stepped on the bandwagon with many thousands who stop obsessive sex habits. She did it with all-or-nothing zeal. She informed her husband sex was not their life-support system anymore, though it had been for a long time.

"We'll live on communication," she stated. She thought cutting off her marital oxygen tube would make all the difference and it did—for a month. Then she noticed a big change in her husband. He used to do small favors for her—wash her car; bring her flowers; call her during the work day. He had even done things he hated to do such as grocery shopping, mall shopping and visiting her relatives. Truth was, Liz's husband was willing to do most anything to please her since sex was their first and last form of communication each day. Waking up with sex and going to bed with it was her husband's idea of romance. Some romance.

Well, that died. Now he wasn't so generous. He sent no flowers and didn't call her at work. He no longer sacrificed his time, energy and money on shopping trips. In short, Liz's husband turned into a regular ogre. She resented him for it at first. She figured he'd only wanted her for orgasm. A receptacle for his morning and nightly deposits.

Liz was furious. She thought she was purely a sex object manipulated by her husband's conceited habits. Her resentment turned bitter and she seriously considered divorce. "That will teach him not to see me as a sex slave," she thought.

Elizabeth never looked inward until she sat and talked to her husband about why he was different. After dodging the topic, he confessed, "I don't know any other way to show you love and affection. That's all we ever did; we were sex mates, not really friends."

His statement hit her like a thunderbolt—not really friends? Not even acquaintances? Liz finally realized her sex mania fabricated a relationship that never had a solid base—a roof, maybe, but no foundation. She was appalled at how their house of cards disintegrated into dust after their hot sex stopped.

They disguised their love, she realized, in ribbons of carnal physical joy that had nothing to do with sharing, caring, or wanting to spend a life together. Liz couldn't debate him. Her husband was right. They shared nothing; they did nothing of substance together except fornicate. Conversations? Never. Discussion about current events? Never. Help with family issues? Rarely. Even their social life was a farce. They looked like the perfect couple. Friends saw them getting along, laughing and affectionate.

"That was our public image." Elizabeth acknowledged to herself. They could play the Barbie-and-Ken marriage around their friends and family. They could plaster on a smile and kid around with each other just as people thought they should. They were products of what people expected them to be.

Without people around they were hollow. At home, they were bored with each other and would spend time independently doing their own thing rather than together. Boredom only went away when they submerged in intense sexual play, magnified by creative fantasy and a mutual willingness to try new, erotic positions.

What did Elizabeth do about this problem? She caved in. She figured, "Hey, I can't afford to lose my marriage." Since she didn't want to lose her husband, she decided that frequent sex was better than living a dull life with him or an even duller life without him.

Put Liz in the penalty box. She sold her soul to the devil way too early in the fight. You may wonder if Elizabeth did everything she could to preserve her new lifestyle? Was the pressure too stiff and her needs too great? Did she even put up a minor struggle? No. Elizabeth hated the change and worried herself to death about the one thing you'll learn to overcome—*fear of a new life*.

This chapter talks about many possible pitfalls that trip you along your path of recovery. Expect them; look for them; even experience them if you must, but only temporarily. You'll fight off pitfalls better than Elizabeth did since you'll have the code that breaks through roadblocks. Be sure to use your codes, your skills, and insights as much as you need to. Never assume setbacks mean your efforts are ineffectual. Make them, instead, learning experiences and suddenly your healthy sexuality will endure.

It Hurts Too Much

Elizabeth surrendered too early. So did Jarek, but for a different reason. Jarek saw his nonsexual life as unfulfilling and blamed his spouse of 15 years for being frigid. He said it was her fault:

"She doesn't know how to perform sex. She lies there and lets me do it, but that's it. It's like having sex with a corpse." He lamented over boring sex. "I make the advances. I do the foreplay-if you can call it that-and even beg her to try new positions." Complaint after complaint—Jarek found nothing redeeming about his wife's sexuality. He wanted a change. He wanted a thrill. If his wife wouldn't come through, he'd find somebody else.

For Jarek, sex life was do or die. He decided moderation in sex was for the birds; his wife was nonorgasmic; and it was time to end the marriage. He thought, it hurts too much to be different; I would rather stay the same and find somebody else who will be a better match.

Jarek figured that somebody new had to be more sexually exciting and challenging. He fantasized about it daily. "I can picture it," he would say. "She is tall, well stacked on top, and can't keep her hands off me. She will want to have sex at least twice a day, maybe more. Yes, many more times and her electricity during coitus will be explosive. I'll be a slave to her consuming erotic passion. I'll be unable to pull myself away."

Jarek's elaborate fantasy world put Disneyland to shame. He constructed the perfect mental mistress to meet his specifications. Now that he knows what he wants, he sets his mind to find it somewhere.

Jarek talked himself into picking erotic fruit from the forbidden garden because he didn't like himself in his new lifestyle. The pain of change made him angry. It devoured his self-esteem and deluded him into perceiving himself as a bad lover.

Jarek absolutely insisted that *pain was insane*. He knew his nonsexual outlook would take time, so he did a 180° turn in his life. He knew blocking urges for sexual gratification would destroy one set of habits to be replaced by uncomfortable, almost bizarre-feeling habits. Jarek knew what he was getting into when he said, "I'm going to cut down on sex." However, he had a short-memory so he forgot how hard it was going to be. He pictured sailing through this change like everything else in his life—but not this time. This time he encountered pain unlike any other pain he ever felt before—the pain of breaking addictive habits. Blocking his sex cravings wasn't much fun.

The more pain he had, the more emotionally withdrawn he was toward his wife, and the more emotionally eager he was toward other women. That is why Jarek and everyone who takes this sex detoxification route must see what pain really is and what it really is not.

Pain in not insane; pain is gain.
There are pain principles for battling undercurrents of sexual arousal. The principles read like this:
1. Pain reminds me I'm hurting because I'm still doing old sex habits.
2. Pain means I'm in transition. I'm leaving one lifestyle and beginning a new, nonsexually consumed lifestyle.
3. Pain is a ticket to relief. Pain tells me a light is at the end of the tunnel and I will be different. Pain navigates me there and gauges whether I'm closer or farther from my sex-change goals.
4. Pain means I'm very aware of what is going on in my mind and body. I'm tapped into my brain's circuit of right and wrong and can make choices I could never make before.
5. Pain proves I'm trying; I feel myself struggling against inner voices that say, "Go back and be the way you were." Pain assures me I'm doing the right thing. It's like a coach cheering me onto victory.

Gain with pain is not easy if you consider any change in your life. It takes time, effort, and most important, it takes commitment. Breaking old commitments to let new ones form violates a comfort zone you'd rather protect. Nevertheless, as you erode this comfort zone, risking a new you, you find pain is no longer the enemy. Pain becomes your friend. Like any trusted companion, pain is a constant reminder that debilitating habits can return and ruin your recovery. As long as some pain is felt, you can rest assured you will not regress back to zero and have to start all over again.

Others Want Me to do Bad Things

Battling rebellious voices inside you is only half the struggle. You can win against yourself just by refocusing on pain as an asset, not a liability. What if people around you put on pressure so heavy you want to call it quits? You'll remember that was Elizabeth's dichotomy. "Should I listen to my instincts of recovery or cut my losses and appease my husband before it's too late and we divorce?" Temptation pulls you both ways like a tug-a-war; either direction you go is bound to have serious emotional results.

Still, unsympathetic people you think are sabotaging your healthy improvement are *not* sabotaging you. You may feel they are. You may even produce proof they undermined your efforts and want you to fail. Inside, you may feel you're fighting a losing battle against these traitors—people who said they loved you and now betray that love.

Jerry's girlfriend was one of these people. At least, Jerry swore she was. He fully believed she was the anti-Christ sent by Lucifer himself to utterly destroy his striving efforts to stop excess sex. She would badger him on the phone at night to come over for sex. He would say "No" but it wouldn't matter. She would accuse him of being queer. She would say, "You're just 'light in the loafers'." She teased him about losing an erection and not being man enough to make love to her. Jerry didn't like hearing all that. He hated thinking of himself as weak and unmasculine.

Jerry's girlfriend—if you listen to Jerry—sounds like a terror and quite possibly his girlfriend was this brutal. After all, Jerry was honestly doing well for himself and then along came this Judas to spoil his gains. Come on, Jerry, is this one-way street? Is all the fuss coming from Jerry's girlfriend? What about Jerry? Is he doing anything wrong? If it takes two to fight, who really threw the first punch? Jerry insists she did.

He's wrong. Jerry knows one thing he's forgetting to tell—wanting sex all the time (addiction) is an escape from facing your own problems and a world of imperfection. Not sure about that? Answer "YES" or "NO" to the following questions:

1. Are you easily upset when things don't go your way? ☐YES ☐ NO
2. Do you think most of your problems are caused by somebody else? ☐YES ☐ NO
3. Do you see yourself a victim, a loser in this battle? ☐YES ☐ NO
4. Do you feel like quitting when the odds are stacked against you? ☐YES ☐ NO
5. Do you get over small setbacks in a few minutes? ☐YES ☐ NO
6. Do you hate people talking about you behind your back? ☐YES ☐ NO
7. Do you think people are conspiring against you at work or home? ☐YES ☐ NO
8. Do you make it a personal policy not to trust people? ☐YES ☐ NO
9. Do you hate to admit you did anything wrong? ☐YES ☐ NO
10. If you show your weaknesses, do you think people will step all over you? ☐YES ☐ NO

Count up your answers. Ten out of ten answered with "Yes?" Maybe some of you scored a couple of "No's" but the majority of answers were "YES?" The good news is that you understood the questions correctly.

The bad news is that all "YES" scores mean you need a scapegoat. You're looking for a stool pigeon to blame for all of your hideous mistakes in recovering from sex addiction. No matter how much you confess the pain of recovery hurts, you would rather accuse another person of hurting you more. People external to you become the target of vengeance. You feel you must get back at them for what they did to you and what they made you become—a sex maniac.

Now it's payback time—sweet revenge. Every ounce of hurt you experienced is turned into missiles of hatred propelled against people close to you. Don't spare anybody—girlfriends, boyfriends, parents, parents-in-laws, and even children. Count them all in. You feel they are all responsible for robbing you of a normal, healthy life and *making* you go through this lousy change in lifestyle.

Other people cannot make you want to do bad things. They can't *make* you do anything. You blame certain people for *making* you be the person you can't accept in yourself. Rather than having ingested your own poison, you're saying they intravenously inject the poison in you. You're deflecting your intolerance of your faults from you to them.

You'll have to do what seems impossible to overcome this backwards perception. First, pretend everything about you from your physical appearance to your thoughts is in a picture on a wall and you are looking at it—not a mirror, a picture on a wall. Look at your picture as a detached object. Now, critique that picture just as you would a picture in a museum or gallery. Don't be polite. Name every flaw and mistake your eyes see—it's too tall, too fat, too slow, too angry, too stupid. Go into detail. Write your impressions below. Do it now.

Flaws I see when I see myself like a picture

1. _____
2. _____
3. _____
4. _____
5. _____
6. _____
7. _____
8. _____
9. _____
10. _____

Now that you have a list, remind yourself that the picture is about you, not somebody else. All of those disturbing flaws belong to one and only one person—YOU. You put them up there and you've amplified them loud and clear so there is no mistaking the identity.

Own them. These imperfections are yours. As you embrace these shortcomings, tell yourself why you have them. Be honest about your past and exactly why your sex cravings got out of hand. Hear yourself say, for example;

➢ *I was greedy for pleasure.*
➢ *I was impulsive and always wanted what I wanted.*
➢ *I hated myself and wanted a quick way to feel good about myself.*
➢ *I was never patient.*
➢ *I was addicted to approval and would do anything for it.*

These are valid reasons for creating flaws. Flaws you put on the table for your eyes only are the first step to affirmation. You're affirming you are the author of many mistakes causing sex maniac patterns. Whatever others did just accelerated the preexisting momentum of faults that I perpetrated. I am this defective person who loved sex for sex. I can't blame anybody but myself, no matter how much I want to.

Self-blame is not a guilt trip, nor is it a pity-party. You're hitting yourself below the belt so you can realize the best thing in the world. When you fully own mistakes—see that picture of flaws as your own—you're taking responsibility for not only what you did, but what you *can do in the future*. By deflecting imperfections back onto yourself, you return to the driver's seat. You're in control again—real control. The type of control where changes you make are by you, for yourself.

In the past that's not what "control" meant to you. Then it meant making people do what you wanted them to do or making people feel what you wanted them to feel. Not anymore. Now you're not controlling others, you're controlling yourself.

Step two is to accept your faults as the NEW YOU. That's right. Believe it or not, the new you is not a perfect specimen. It's made up of so many mistakes there's no way of purifying it. You can't single out all of the imperfections, sterilize them, and end up with a fault-free specimen.

No, you're stuck with every last blemish in your personality and, to tell you the truth, that's the way it should be. Flaws you learn to accept are the normal self you can become.

Be proud of that self. Don't lock it away in the closet and throw away the key. Bring it out in the foyer of your mind and step into it until you feel yourself absorbed by these faults. No, you're not slipping into some evil trance or a deception meant to trick you, you're coming to grips with the part of you hidden from the surface through fear of facing it.

The third step allows you to step inside the picture you created of yourself with flaws and pretend you are that picture. No longer are you a spectator viewing the picture on the wall, now you've become the picture. Enter it as if you're stepping onto a bus. Feel the deluge of tension as you allow yourself to feel imperfect and realize there's no escape from imperfection. You're in this together—you and the picture. No two separate entities anymore—just one.

Life Won't Be Fun

Party time—number one activity on your list? Perhaps like Frank and Sherri. They led the pack of party animals from the word go. Two working parents raising three kids put a huge strain on their marriage.

Fridays, watch out! They dropped the kids off at either Frank's or Sherri's parents, then made a bee-line to "Happy Hour." The couple were regulars at Sammy's Bar and Grill, (A local restaurant-tavern perfect for business get-a-ways).

Frank looked forward to Fridays for another reason. After guzzling one or two beers, he and Sherri would dash back to the house and aggressively have sex. Sherri didn't spare the graphic details. "We frantically tore into each other, like dogs in heat, rolling on the bed with hot passion."

Frank explained something else. "When it is over," he insisted, "believe me, it is something special to remember." The animalistic chemistry between Frank and Sherry made every Friday afternoon a powerful erotic experience—lubricated, of course, with several beers. Liquor is a stress-reducer for them but in a distinct way. It lit them up like firecrackers, bursting in erotically, compulsive rituals until they reached their euphoria— the climax. Once at orgasm, both were drained. They melted into a state of utter exhaustion and fell asleep for the night.

Their Friday rituals did more than promise a sexual paradise. It meant they could tolerate the frustrating work week knowing how much fun Friday would be. Frank and Sherri aren't dummies—they hit the nail on the head in describing their sexual hangups. "We do it as a safe escape and it's better than using drugs." They are right. They use no cocaine, no marijuana, no street pills. Even alcohol intake is marginal (one to two beers) and restricted to Friday afternoons. They smoke cigarettes but less than a pack a day. In their eyes, "we're relatively drug-free."

However, their Friday rendezvous wasn't a drug issue—it was a fun-issue. Sex became a giant M&M®. Driven by compulsive urges and high intensity physical lovemaking, they relied on Fridays. They were not only pure entertainment, but also a security blanket. It was therapy. They knew any arguments they had Monday through Thursday would be cured on Friday. Any headaches, stomach aches or nail-biting tensions suffered before or after hump day (Wednesday) would be released. Fridays meant the world to them. Frank and Sherri worshiped Fridays as a holy day—guaranteed to wash away their sins and purify them again to face another grueling week with work and children.

Fridays were *fun and necessary*. Sex was not romance, it was a drug for Frank and Sherri and that's what they explicitly wanted to stay away from. They were proud to say, "We don't do drugs." The truth is, they did. Sex became feverishly addictive. It's sedative properties sterilized their mind and body after being aggressively pumped up by alcohol and indulgent love-making. The problem they faced was, what would happen to their fun when addictive sex stopped?

Fun evaporated from their lives, not because they didn't know how to have fun, but because their only fun revolved around their Friday sexual jubilees. Happiness is like that. Those who put all of their joy and happiness in one activity deeply rely on that activity. Kill the activity and consequently fun vanishes.

When Frank and Sherri took a nonsex maniac vow, changing their habits so they tenderly made love instead of rutting as animals in heat, Fridays vanished. They didn't have a clue about what to do with each other or, for that matter, how to be affectionately romantic.

This is their solution: Diversity and flexibility. I call it the "D-F" principle. It goes like this:

D=Diversity—be playful in as many situations as possible instead of restricting play to one or two situations.

F=Flexibility—be open and adaptable in old and new situations so you can be yourself and be playful. Never turn a good thing into a solid routine or ritual. Once you do, it stops you from being creative with play in new situations.

Frank and Sherri got the gist of this principle. They agreed to try an experiment. Tuesdays and Fridays they would skip the booze and spend the evening with their children After the kids went to bed, they watched a video and had a snack together. Before going to bed, they either had sex or shared tidbits about their week.

However, they did not carve the order of activities-play with kids, video, snack, sex or discussion-in stone. Sometimes they were robotic with the order—other times they varied it. First the snack, then some conversation—sometimes they even skipped sex. They got into the business of flexibility and saw its obvious advantages.

They said, "We're not locked into something we gotta do." Not being locked in meant they had many chances during the week to release frustrations and be happy. They didn't stuff their frustrations for an entire week before recklessly exploding them in sexual aggression. Now, they release their frustrations a little at a time, at different times, in different ways. Play isn't a once-a-week thing. Play was as little or as much as they wanted it to be.

It's Like Going to Mars

Frank and Sherri are like the rest of us. You pull yourself out of the trap of strong habits and begin a lifestyle that feels weird. So odd, in fact, you think you have gone to Mars. Pack up your old routines, the things you loved but can't do; the thoughts you had that weren't good for you; the sex you enjoyed that turned addictive.

All these intimate parts of your personality undergo transformation. It is as if you're in a cocoon in the midst of a spectacular metamorphosis and you can't stop the motion of things changing. You advance from what you were and who you were but you may not know where you're going and what you'll be like when you get there.

You need a reliable roadmap as you change sex habits and head for the stars. Altering the inner you is going into an unexplored galaxy. You know the parameters, you basically know what you can and cannot do and you know your limitations. Nevertheless, within these limitations—these boundaries—lies a world of untapped potentials waiting for you to excavate them and put them to good use.

Potential abilities inside you almost always can be found using the right treasure map. As on any map, longitudinal and latitudinal coordinates direct you to the exact spot where your strengths are buried.

Here are the personal coordinates you can use to rapidly find the new you. See how each of the following steps reveals a side of yourself you thought didn't exist.

Coordinates to Take You Through the Transition to Healthy Sex

Three steps will enable you to resist temptation and discover wonders of healthy sex.

1. **Sensitivity.** Sensitivity is being in tune with your own and somebody else's feelings. If your prevalent feeling is guilt, it means you are experiencing shame. Think about it, then ask yourself where it recently originated. Trace its short-roots to words you said or action you performed that caused conflict. If the guilt is over being sexually healthy—such as your partner pressuring for more sex when you want less sex— accept that guilt as normal. Resist fixing the problem. When guilt has nothing to do with sex, explore why it happened and what you can do about it.

   Sensitivity is listening to your inner hurt and the hurt of others and sharing what you hear.

2. **Be a caretaker.** Usually, caretaking is unwanted. A caretaker—in the language of relationships—means a person who appeases another person at his or her own expense and ultimately feels used. Usually, caretakers feel very little self-worth and live entirely through trying to make another person or persons feel happy. Happiness for the caretaker depends on happiness for the person to whom they give care. With sex maniacs, it's a different story. You are not the usual type of caretaker. You need to unselfishly sublimate your emotions or your personal agenda to give your partner 100% of your kindness. That would be pleasant, but can it happen? Usually, your partner gets 20% or less of your love—you take the rest. That's not caretaking.

   Pure caretaking is just the opposite—you give 80% to 90% of your love and settle with the remainder.

   When you are a caretaker, you're...
   - ➤ Asking how a person feels and lending your ear of compassion.
   - ➤ Doing things for another person unexpectedly and without reminders.

> Yielding to another person's decision or opinion even when you disagree.
> Wholeheartedly doing something for another person from whom you gain, maybe, a thank-you.

Attempts at being a caretaker do more than you think. You don't turn into a pure caretaker; you turn into a *delightful person who does caretaking things*. Help that you give to another person helps yourself. You discover how simple it is to balance impulsively-driven selfish needs with generosity. The two skills together form a stronger you and a more likable person.

3. **Give unconditional love.** Benevolently being there for people is tough. You have to really want to please another person without any strings attached. That's what *unconditional love* means. It is the bedrock of healthy sexual behavior. You donate your genius in lovemaking to another person and do not expect to get anything in return. It's as if you planted and harvested a crop but don't eat it. Sure, occasionally you can partake of the crop but only in moderation.

You give unconditional love when you do the following:
> You spend time with somebody without sexual advances or actual intercourse.
> You buy gifts for a person to show your affection and refuse to accept a gift in return.
> You praise and encourage a person for what they've done when their achievements have nothing at all to do with you.
> You remind a person frequently of your love for them, knowing they may or may not respond in kind.

Sensitivity, caretaking, and unconditional love move you in leaps and bounds from whom you were to what you want to become. You can only discover this passage by actually trying. Start tonight, not tomorrow to be a nonsex maniac. See what happens when sex is a peripheral thought in your mind. Instead, place in the forefront loving—not *lovemaking*, compassion— not *passion*, self-control— not *self-indulgence*.

Tonight and all the days and nights ahead are waiting for you to begin. Just do it. Don't let yourself down.

Chapter Five
The New You

Melissa looked at herself in the mirror. She saw the same person with the same face, same hands, same body—everything she was used to but something was different.

Every morning for the last ten years Melissa had looked at herself in the mirror. Every morning in those last ten years she had asked herself how good her sex with her husband Rick had been the night before

She played judge and jury. A verdict of "guilty" made her sulk in depression. She would ruin her day ruminating over what she did wrong and how it displeased Rick. A verdict of "not guilty" still didn't spare her. Even if Melissa figured her aerobic energy and filthy eroticism pleased Rick, she'd always find a reason to be critical. She would think, Yes, but he didn't…

…tell me he loved me.
…show as much excitement.
…thank me for what I did for him.
…ask me if I wanted an orgasm.
…really think I was worth it.

Rick never did any of these things. That's why Melissa finally kicked the habit. Until today she stared into the mirror overanalyzing her sex habits to death, and plunged herself deeper into depression.

After ten years, she got tired of this ordeal and stopped thinking and talking about her sex life. She stopped worrying and scheming about making Rick's penis happy. It was his, not hers, so let him worry about how it feels.

When she stopped altogether, Melissa became a nonsex maniac.

The mirror saw a different person as she faced each new day. It wasn't the same Melissa. Oh, sure, physically it was, but not mentally. The new Melissa wanted to think positively about her physical attraction, her skills, her benefits to herself and her family. Melissa wanted to free herself of the courtroom trial of her sexual performance.

Slowly, but with great persistence, she did just that. This chapter describes the finishing touches Melissa—and many other people like her—perform when they've accepted a nonsex maniac life. These are the ways they insure their efforts are permanent. They plant skills like perennials to return every day, every year, and every time you need them.

You become your own maintenance person. The "maintenance" steps are not really difficult but they do take a personal commitment to follow through with yourself. As Melissa looking in the mirror, you can stop your rituals by first knowing you have those rituals. Second, by knowing how to interrupt and replace those rituals. Third, change occurs when you make the New You as natural as you can in your life.

How to Like the New You

Being different doesn't mean you'll like who you are. Old habits die hard. You'll vividly remember many good times you had in sexual paradise. Those chunks of good memories are deceiving. You'll be deceived at first. You'll say to yourself, "If it were a good memory, it must have been something good." It's tempting to believe that but what you remember as good today may not have been wonderful yesterday. For example, you may still remember your Sunday evening rituals at college.

Craig and Jeremy sure do. They would finish studying for a test and get together about dinner time. The dorm cafeteria didn't serve food on Sunday, so they were on their own for dinner.

"Here's what we did," Jeremy recalls. "About 5:30 P.M. or so, Craig and I would turn on the TV for background noise. We would undress and snuggle under the covers. It felt great. Then—and here was the best part—Craig would massage my front and backside. Talk about sensuous, this scored a 10+. It felt euphoric and I lost myself in the sensations. Of course, I'd do the same for Craig."

Craig agreed with the excitement, adding his own version to the story, "Here's what Jeremy did—if you can believe it. He'd start to wash my genitals, both with his mouth and then a sponge. I think I enjoyed the oral sex more. I've never tingled so much in my life."

Craig meant it. He'd been around the bar scene with lovers but never experienced such passion until meeting Jeremy.

Their highly erotic tales of what they used to do Sunday college nights sounded memorable. At first they couldn't recall why they stopped this ritual, since every detail was positive. Except for one thing, it was pure ecstasy.

Jeremy remembered what it was. "We always argued viciously the next day."

Jeremy explained how great they felt after sex. They slept arm in arm, fitted together perfectly like a glove and hand. However, no sooner did they wake up than Craig or Jeremy got cranky. A minor squabble escalated in seconds. They lost their tempers and exploded into angry volcanic rages. Craig would call Jeremy a slut; Jeremy would jealously accuse Craig of sleeping with other guys. The turbulence grew until they physically punched each other.

"That's why we stopped." they said as they suddenly remembered why they hated their Sunday ritual. This is what they concluded together: *Rituals don't work if they produce problems that can ruin not only the ritual but also everything the ritual hoped to gain.*

Craig and Jeremy became nonsex maniacs. They still had sex and found it mutually stimulating but they deliberately became more spontaneous and playful. They had no compulsive routines and no set rules for enjoying each other's carnal company. Sex left its ritualistic status and became a free-spirited, healthy game of enjoyment.

Craig and Jeremy maintained their non-routine sex life by teaching themselves how to like what they were doing. They wanted an ironclad system to keep both of them on task, focused, and not prone to relapse. Neither trusted each other's word. A promise was great but not very reliable. They needed something more, something more solid. A concrete solution had to be employed. They found one in the *Like Yourself Inventory(LYI)*. The LYI is a nifty device used for rapid reassurance. It's a self-booster, a power-motivator, and self-monitor. It also reminds you of why your current change in habits is working so well and what you can realistically expect in days ahead being a nonsex maniac.

Here's how the inventory works. Follow the steps below to see what the overall effect is for you.

LYI—Your Personal Validity Tool

1. On a piece of paper, quickly list five things of which you are proud. List the things you started doing in the last month or since taking the oath of nonsex maniac.
2. For each of these five, answer the following questions:
    A. Could you do these things before the NEW YOU?
    ☐ YES ☐ NO
    B. Did you do anything as good as these things before the NEW YOU?
    ☐ YES ☐ NO
    C. When you do these things, do you feel sad or angry?
    ☐ YES ☐ NO

D. When you do these things, do you think about wanting sex?
   ☐ YES ☐ NO
   E. When you do these things, does your body feel horny?
   ☐ YES ☐ NO
   (Let's hope you've answered each question with a "NO.")
3. For each of the five items you listed as being proud of, write an answer for the following questions on that same piece of paper:
   A. How many times a day do you do one, two or all of these proud things?
   B. How many times do people notice it and compliment you?
   C. How many nights a week do you go to bed feeling rested, happy, and emotionally secure?
   D. How many times do you see these proud things pop up at your work, school or when socializing?

What you have done with the *Like Yourself Inventory* is bond with yourself. You came to grips with uplifting facts about the NEW YOU that convince yourself that you are the person you want to be- free from obsession; free from sexual compulsion; and free from turning your life into a sex factory. You are the CEO of your life. You own it, run it, and can make any changes you consider essential to guarantee healthy sexual thoughts and healthy sexual behavior.

Showcase Your Good Points

Want to brag? Okay, do it. It's not a crime although many people insist it is. You've heard stories of lying, pompous individuals who spout off everything good about themselves. They never find a shred of fault. Is it because they are infallible? Do they possess a "perfect" gene we'd die for?

Don't believe it. Pompous braggarts tattle about others and pump up their own ego to try to create something out of nothing. They know what really exists within them-zero. Don't look for brains in a boaster. You won't find any. They talk a good game but don't deliver on promises.

When you think about bragging, is this the stereotype you're faced with? Will they picture you, too, as an egomaniac full of hot air? Many think so. They believe bragging is wrong, immoral, and downright rude. They could be right; maybe it is. You'll only find out if you learn to brag the right way, not the wrong way.

Praising the NEW YOU is not an exercise in arrogance. You're not inflating your ego just for the hell of it. You do it to feel alive and you do it to feel the NEW YOU is an entity; it's not a passing phase. You're not feeling good for a lark, it's real and it's you. The only way to legitimately anchor your genuine feelings into both mind and body is by broadcasting the good news to the world around you. You do this by using self-praise in a subtle manner.

Self-praise is a strategic tool to alert yourself and people around you about how good you feel and why they should feel good about you.

Here are four steps to develop self-praise. They are steps in your transition from compulsive maniac to nonsex maniac:

Step 1. Keep a conversation going by talking about what you like.
Step 2. Shift the conversation to talk briefly about what you like.
Step 3. Initiate a conversation to talk briefly about what you like.
Step 4. Directly solicit feedback on your positive and good qualities.

With Step 1, you keep a conversation going. Wait until somebody else asks you a question, then answer it. As you answer, interject a couple of comments about yourself. You can do the same thing if you enter the conversation of other people. Insert your opinion while referring to something good you did.

For example, if you hear someone say, "Isn't it pleasant outside?" say in reply, "It sure is. I love doing things outside on warm days."

You see, that was simple-nothing pretentious, nothing shockingly conceited. All you did was remark about how much you enjoy the warm weather. At the same time, you provided brief glimpses of who you are and what you like.

Let's try the same tactic regarding a sex topic. Sheila said to Roberta, "I can't sleep without an orgasm."

Roberta answered her: "Yes, I know what you mean. I used to have that problem but now I go to sleep without the orgasm so I don't depend on it as if it is a tranquilizer."

In Step 2, you shift the conversation. A friendly exchange of words gets the engine running. Politely interjecting a positive word or two about you as a person is not harmful. You can also politely conclude the conversation and introduce a new topic. Begin the new topic with a soft remark to gently end one conversation before you start a new one. Then introduce a statement about yourself.

Sasha was complaining about her boyfriend's starvation for sex. "He can't get enough and it drives me crazy."

Jasmen cut her off at the pass, but with tact. "Yes, I know what you mean. Hey, I have to tell you that Gary and I get along great now, since we have sex once a week."

This sentence is about Jasmen, not about Sasha's miserable sex troubles. You may think shifting the conversation is insensitive. After all, you did interrupt Sasha when she was still talking, right?

Right, but that's what everybody does and now you'll do it, too. Interrupting is not imposing. You're not violating the sacred law of the Talmud. You're doing what people have done to you for years, and you didn't know why they did it. *They interrupted you because they wanted to steal your thunder and take center stage for a moment of glory.*

The only drawback to shifting the conversation may be Sasha's utter disbelief that you cut her off. Say, "I'm sorry," and continue with your new topic.

Using Step 3, you can initiate a conversation. Get the ball rolling by inviting people to talk about a topic about you. "Hey, guys, I'll bet you can't guess what Mark and I don't do any more?"

Heads turn and curiosity is aroused. Now go for it. "We don't drink before we have sex, we're into it naturally."

The topic is underway. Comments fly in from all directions, some agreeing, some disagreeing and others are neutral. Overall, they are filling the gaps with ideas initiated by your plug about yourself and how your life has changed.

With Step 4, you directly solicit feedback. You say, "Why don't we skip the polite formalities and just get down to basics. What do you think about Jerry and I talking more and lovemaking less?"

A bold question thrown into the lion's den for feedback. A risky tactic that could get you eaten alive by nasty critics or feed you the sweet sugar of sympathetic pleasers.

Your choice, if you had a choice but you don't. When it comes to soliciting feedback, you're stuck with whatever comes your way.

Polite remarks are naturally better. Guarantee a polite remark by first complimenting the person to whom you're talking. "I am impressed with how you and Janice get along so well. I think Harold and I are doing better as well."

Slick, eh? You cleverly slid in that tidbit about yourself after lubricating the playing field with an M&M® for the listener. They loved it. They ate it up. Feed them plenty of M&M's® as they continue to listen to your questions.

That's what it takes to solicit people for opinions. Be soft toward them and they will be soft toward you. In response, you'll get honesty, friendship, and direct input about your achievements. Best of all, you'll hear yourself announcing your good qualities on the social loudspeaker. As you hear them, you'll believe them. They will sink in as truth. Your achievements are true! You did them, didn't you?

Be a Leader, Be a Helper

You have built up the nerve to speak your piece. You interject remarks that could be construed as slightly boastful- maybe more than slightly. You're a helper and a sounding board. You can blend into any conversation and add your two-cents without feeling self-conscious. Quite an accomplishment.

Being a helper in conversations is an asset. You keep the dialogue moving, give sympathy, empathy, and stir the pot of opinions, both about yourself and others. However, that's about it. Your lifespan as helper is short because there is only so much you can do.

Therefore, nonsex maniacs try to be leaders. They are educators, teachers, and coaches. They unload their triumphs in an amiable style using the showcase method discussed above. Leaders proudly explain their control of sex and the torrential rainstorm they went through to finally achieve it. They are not bashful. Shy achievers, you see, are not achievers. They think they are but are uncertain if they've really achieved anything. When you've earned a victory, you know it. You feel compelled to share it. You want people to know that not only did you do it, but *they can do it also.*

Make no mistake about it though, nonsex maniacs are not a religion. They do not identify a higher power as the reason for their personal gains. Spiritually they may believe in a God or Prophets of God and use their faith to support them through turbulent withdrawal from sex compulsions. In the end, where faith guided them, it was the sex maniac himself or herself who met the standards. You are to be rewarded for what you did. Nobody did it for you; nobody made you do it; and nobody could stand in your way.

You are the sole crusader of your voyage from the dark side of sex compulsions to the freedom of healthy sexual habits. You did it with your own pride, no matter who or what shared the pride with you.

Make it Stick

Eric didn't start as a hero. He didn't know what freedom from sex compulsions meant. How could he? He was too deep in emotional debt. He had lost his girlfriend and was on the verge of losing his job all because he couldn't break his habit-he loved computers.

No, he wasn't a cybersurfing freak-internet journeys were only his hobby. He wasn't hooked on webpage browsing. Eric had one passion that preoccupied his mind and drove him into lost time. He spent hours in search of the perfect euphoria- Cybersex.

Eric admitted his addiction was on-line sex in chat-rooms and e-mail. He'd log on after work and skip meals while he cruised desperately for homosexual and heterosexual partners willing to exchange graphically explicit, verbal foreplay.

Once found, he buzzed through keystrokes, typing e-mail after e-mail to respondents who would promise him anal and oral sex. He replied in elaborate detail about how he would stimulate their genitals and be a slave to their sexual fantasies. Pressing for sado-masochistic replies, Eric didn't stop at heavy verbal foreplay. He described himself being whipped, stung, and inflicted with other pain, inviting readers to bite the bait.

Hundreds of instant replies came in. They described how Eric could make them reach orgasm. They would cut him with a knife; they would twist his penis until he yelled; they would stick their penis deeply into his mouth, nearly choking him. As if that wasn't bad enough, Eric got replies about being shot, maimed, and hung.

Eric consumed this X-rated erotica with a voracious appetite until he nearly lost his job from staying up so long and then being too tired to go to work. His girlfriends all left him. They complained of his computer addiction and strange experimental sex habits with them. He tried to live out cyberfantasies during their lovemaking. Of course, it would fail miserably and Eric, deep in imagination, didn't have a clue about what he did wrong to his partners.

Eric's world of make-believe came to a screeching halt during a thunderstorm when his power was out. He hadn't anticipated what would happen if he had to go a night without online orgasm. When it did happen, Eric suffered excruciating misery the entire night as his sexual cravings went through withdrawal.

In the morning, Eric felt ashamed and stupid. He realized how wasteful his life had been. He had been plugged into sexual illusion and wishful thinking. He decided then and there to abstain from cybersex and begin anew. He would look to people for his heterosexual needs.

Eric's steps in recovery are still underway. He has not made it yet but he sticks with his sex control by mentally rehearsing four "I can do" statements. These are like prayers. They remind you of your belief in yourself and the courage it takes to overcome painfully, destructive habits. Eric reads them aloud to himself every night because he can't afford to forget them. You won't want to forget them either.

➢ I can do anything if I try. Trying is magic for my self-confidence.
➢ I can do things I've never done before. Doing is being brave and taking a risk.
➢ I can do things people say I can't do. People don't know the inner me. I do.
➢ I can do whatever it takes to reach my goal. My goals are real. I make them real by seeing them happen every day of my life.

The same as in Alcoholics Anonymous, becoming a nonsex maniac is a one-step-at-a-time process. You and your habits go to bat each time normal sexual cravings arise. You decide if sex is right or should occur in appropriate ways. You condone or condemn it. You let it happen or pull the plug on it. Within your grasp is the executive navigating power to engineer healthy sex drives.

Conducted correctly, sex becomes a pleasant experience equally shared between you and your partner. Performed even better, sex is the product of passion, romance, and sensuous intimacy where you and your partner spend quality time *being together.*

Sex is not just a physical act. Sex is the time, effort and energy invested in loving another person. From touching to verbally complimenting, when sex happens, it is the finale of a precious bond.

Unlike alcohol, sex is not something you abstain from-you need it and you do deserve it. Humans are a species who love to play with their reproductive organs. You can learn self-love or love of another using sex when impulses are kept in moderation and you expand your boundary of life experiences.

This book guided you through life expansion. It showed you there is hope. You can easily and rapidly stop your addictive sex habits by altering the habits and becoming a nonsex maniac. You'll view life as nonsex maniacs do-life does not revolve around your next orgasm. Life is diverse. One day you may have sex; another day you may not. It all depends on how flexible and spontaneous you allow yourself to be.

No matter how much progress you made, one thing should be blatantly clear by now. Sex is addictive. It can be destructive. You can lose yourself in this mesmerizing search for the perfect climax.

Spare yourself the grief-be the real you. The you who was healthy in childhood; the you who enjoyed simple things and wanted simple love. Don't make life unnecessarily complex and delude yourself into thinking that sex is the gateway to solving this complexity. It isn't. It complicates it more.

Take the skills you've learned thus far and restore your true self. Show yourself you can do it and watch others admire your incredible speed of recovery. How fast you go and how much you dedicate your life to healthy sex depends on your inner voice. Hear yourself say, "I am worth it," and watch your progress soar.

However, that's only the beginning. Tell yourself, "I am worthy of love for love itself, and not for the physical love I expect." With these words you'll solidly anchor your recovery in cement. It will never waver and you will be at peace with yourself and your partner forever.

Chapter Six
Use Condoms: A Warning about Diseases and Aids

While it is normal and healthy to enjoy an active sex life, partners may feel reticent to advance beyond smooching without proof that you are safe. Sure, you may be trustworthy, reliable, and responsible. Good; you've made it half way to their hearts. But nowadays proof is by verdict only. Partners want absolute iron-clad guarantees you are not infected with a nasty sexually transmittable disease (STDs). And there's over 30 STDs you can catch to make matters worse. You may feel you're safe, even insist you've been with honest clean partners, but statistics say otherwise.

PEOPLE LIE!

Safe sex performed with safe people largely depends on the honor code. What you say may be true, but I wouldn't count on 100% of what's told to you. Sexually eager types, especially, may tell a fib. They may or may not be checked of health risks and they figure a one-time encounter won't spoil the fun. How can I get infected after sex one time?

Easily. It happens all the time. You are not immune. *The only thing that is immune is your mind. If you pretend your body is safe, you can believe your body is safe. Problem is, the illusion only lasts so long.*

Discovery of STDs on you is probably the most miserable form of humiliation. Your partner may discover it or you may uncover symptoms of a disease. And there's no way on this Earth your partner will consent to anything remotely sexual until that disease is gone and your body passes a health inspection. That's why it pays to know what these buggers are, what they look like, and general treatment for them. Among the ten most devastating and common STDs circulating the dating world include:

Disease	*Symptoms*	*Treatment*
chlamydia	pain, burning when urinating;	antibiotic that kills yellow discharge
crabs or public lice	severe itching	prescription or over-the-counter lotions
genital herpes	red bumps, blisters in genital area;	pills & ointments for pain or burning when peeing symptoms but no real cure
genital warts	bumpy warts on or near genitals	removal of warts but no cure HPV inside your anus or vagina
gonorrhea	pain/burning when urinating;	antibiotic that kills bacteria yellow discharge
hepatitis B	yellow skin, abdominal pain,	pills, shots for symptoms, nausea & vomiting but no cure; vaccine

molluscum contagiosum	small white bumps around genital/anal area	removal of bumps but no cure
pelvic inflamed disease (women)	cramping or pain in pelvic or abdominal area	antibiotics
scabies	line of small red spots, very	prescription and itchy over-the counter lotions
syphilis	painless open sores, rash, genital	penicillin shots to ulcers, flu-like symptoms kill bacteria

Prolonged exposure to these diseases may complicate cures. You may discover you've picked up a STD and rush over to the doctors to get a shot or an antibiotic. That took care of you for the time being. But continued sex with your infected partner who is untreated may re-expose you and weaken your body's natural fighting agents (immunities) against these foreign substances. To make matter worse, untreated STDs are not only ugly, itchy, painful and sexually unattractive, you may be increasing your lousy chances of getting cancer. In women, recurrent STDs including repeated yeast infections can cause birth defects in children and be early signs of a horrible disease—HIV.

God, not that one. Please not AIDS. AIDS, or *acquired immune deficiency*, is the final stage of a progressive illness caused by an immunodeficiency virus or HIV. Having this HIV virus *does not mean you have AIDS*. You can be a carrier of HIV and not develop AIDS symptoms. But you may not know you're in the clear until months or years down the road. Symptoms at first are confusing and overlap with other normal colds and flue-like reactions.

Still, it's persistence of certain symptoms that tips you off. You may feel nausea, diarrhea, have unexplained weight loss or fatigue, swollen glands, fever, shaking, or chills lasting more than several weeks, blurred vision, severe headaches, easy bruising, pink to purple blotches, and easily susceptible to other infections particularly lung infection (e.g., Pneumocystis Carinii Pneumonia)

The trouble with AIDS is obvious. It's easy to get and not so easy to cure. In fact, as of this writing, there is no cure. That's why you're advised to prevent contact with the disease instead of spending time, energy and lots of dollars arresting the symptoms once infected.

How can I prevent AIDS and still be sexually active? That's a good question. Public health warnings are pretty Victorian. They say to reduce your number of sexual partners. The thinking being that, if you have sex with one person, you're actually having intercourse with every partner she or he has had. Some thought, eh? It gives new meaning to *menage a toi*. Still, you don't want to throw caution in the wind. There are four things you can reasonably due to safely protect your body and be informed about another person's risk hazard. While not a perfect guarantee, it's better than impulsively flying by the seat of your pants and having unprotected sex. So, how about if you:

- Ask about the health status of your partner. Apologize for sounding like the Surgeon General but get the facts anyway. You can overcome shyness. You can't overcome AIDS.
- Ask to literally see an AIDS health screening test. While it's not bulletin proof, you're a lot smarter and safer given these results than by taking their sweet word on it.
- Avoid sex when you've used drugs or drank alcohol. Don't be stupid. Mind-altering states make you forget your name and phone-number. How the hell are you going to remember to ask questions about AIDS? You're not.
- Avoid contact with body fluids. Well, I know this means say goodbye to fallatio and cunnilingus, to an extent. I wouldn't go for prize-winning sex until you had your facts.
- Guys—wear latex condoms. None of these excuses about you can't feel the natural you. Tough, I'd rather you struggle to keep

an erection while safely wrapped in a rubber suit than to eat the forbidden apple in the Garden of Eden; one lousy weak moment of forgetting to put on a rubber and you'll see how quickly the Garden of Eden looks like a cemetery.

Chapter Seven
Can Sex Be Love?

This book has been about love. A special kind of love. The love between two people in the form of sharing passion, intimacy, and deeply satisfying orgasm. Okay, so that sounds superficial. Love is in a class by itself. You may not want to associate love with a strong climax. But you do, like it or not. It's a pair no matter how you look at it. And if you think love is this innocent Victorian picture of romance, let me tell you; those Victorians were hot lovers. They were just as lewd, crude and full of lust as today's finest barflying couple.

Still don't like how sex is love? I know why; you're stuck on believing that love is different from lovemaking. Passion is different from compassion. One is forever; the other isn't. Sex is short-lasting. It has brief episodes of excitement. And love, you think, sticks to you like an emotional glue. Once stuck, you're affixed for life. With sex, you physically indulge your body to feel a spontaneous thrill. A roller coaster high. Then, poof, it's over. But you say, "No, not love." Love allows your senses to marinate in sweet juices for as long as you'd like.

Love, you think, is better than sex? Is that what love is for you? Really? Good. Then, time to wake up.

It's time to board the clue-train.

You've been duped. You don't have a clue to what you've been doing. What you call romance is built on a meter of affection. How much or how little you get determines love. And every bit of physical affection scores a point. Touching gets 2 points. Kissing a big-3 hooper. French-kissing earns a bonus of 4 points. And you figure the rest. Petting genitals is really racking up the points. As for sex? You've won the lottery of points.

Have you counted your point total today? Has anybody touched you? Kissed you? Petted at least one of your genitals? Did anybody even talk about doing it? Well, do your math.

Zero!

That's right. A big zero for the day. I don't know about you but I don't do *zeros* well. No points, no love. No love, no romance. No romance, no relationship. Math works that easily.

Calculate something else while you're at it. When was the last time your special person, if you have one, verbally complimented you? Last night? Two nights ago?

How about—*I don't remember because it hasn't happened for centuries!*

Love doesn't exist in your mind. It exists in your body. You feel it. You experience it. You starve for it. *You can call whatever you want love, and that's fine. But love is not a thing in itself; it is what results from how you physically and verbally share with another person. And that other person is who this book is about.*

And, of course, let's not forget the obvious. *How you treat somebody depends on how romantic or caring you are toward them.* That's why love and sex go together. And what is worse, sex is pretty selfish. You're not a moral crusader when you do a skydive into carnal bliss. It's a "for-me" crusade. You're daring yourself to discover a higher plateau of ecstasy; if it's higher it's better. Reaching beyond your limits is sensual. It lets you achieve a peak experience and know exactly how far your body can go. And you'd be surprised how far you can go. Men—try having sex five times a night. Women—try having multiple orgasms.

Think it's impossible?

Nothing is impossible. You just have to know what to do and who to do it with.

You just push further and demand more of yourself. Nothing in moderation. You don't want good sex; you want *great sex*. Let it soar uncontrollably. Build up muscle pressure until your body feels like a steam kettle ready to blow. Speed is everything Slow sex doesn't boil the water. Fast and hot does. You fuel your insides with inertia that ultimately explodes in a muscle spasm. Then sensations rush wildly throughout your body, flooding you with euphoria. Sparkles of rainbow colors fill your eyes as you sink into sweet oblivion. It's melody to your ears.

That is, for as long as it lasts. Perfect sex might produce these great feelings. But who has perfect sex? I don't. And you don't either. In fact, if you're like me, you don't have sex at all.

That's why you bought this book. You know there must be a different way. A way to have sex to rekindle romance and love in your life. "Surely some formula must exist."

Well, it does.

No, it's not a medicine.

No, it's not a quick-fix.

And, sorry, it's not a magical spell, hypnosis, or an aphrodisiac.

Good ideas, but they're a bunch of mumbo-jumbo.

You want *real sex? I mean really hot stimulating down-right dirty sex?* Good.

First you have to follow the strategies in previous chapters on having sex in moderation. That way, sex is second, not first in your mind. Then you have to ask yourself: Who is really a healthy sex partner? Is there a partner who won't feed my sex addiction, but who is still desirable? Can I make love to *average sex partners; partners who make sex a second, not a first priority?*

Sex and sex partners are not abstract ideas. You can borrow from the science of human behavior to get clues on which people are receptive and which are resistant to sex. People patterns seem ominous. But they are not. A close inspection of how people behave and why they behave opens the doors to amazing predictions. When you see how these predictions work and understand the formula for figuring out sex partners, you'll be a different person.

You'll feel psychic.

You'll feel like you have a sixth sense able to directly plug into sex-wannabes and know how they think.

You'll feel, for the first time or in a long while, that you can win at SEX JEOPARDY. You'll know what questions to ask in advance, how they may respond, and what to say when they respond.

You'll be incredibly SEX-SMART, with a superior SEX IQ and a real talent for picking and choosing winning partners. Sex partners. Partners who share your dreamscape of healthy arousal. You want it—you get it. It's yours for the asking.

People who tune into your sex signals are not hard to find. They exist out there in society in multiple numbers. Who they are and how to find them is also not a mystery. You just need the right clues to track them down and discern their instinctive needs. Like a good detective, you can collect all of the clues leading directly to your love mate. *How, you ask?*

I'll show you how.

You first have to logically sort out fact from fiction. You may discover stereotypes of sexual people you once thought were true but now are not true at all. Or, people who you assumed hated sex are indeed closet nymphomaniacs. They have more hunger for sex than a bear.

Sex can be a predictable part of your life when you employ the right tactics, for the right reason, at the right time.

Now, does knowing the inside track for sex partners give you permission to be immoral? I mean, will every night be a sex orgy? And, if you're mate isn't putting out, should you trade him or her in for a "Suzie Cream Cheese" or "Brutal-Bob?"

No, don't do that. Not yet. Don't switch lanes on the "No-Passing Zone." You won't have to do that. Insider secrets on locating sex-playmates can give you precious information on how you and your partner can rebuild your sexual life. Real-clues; not fake ones. Forget buying flowers, talking nicely, and making special dinners for you loved one.

Wow, what an effort. That's a wasted investment for no return. Bad planning. With insider sex secrets, you'll know which buttons to push to produce which reactions. But only in moderation; not for kicks; not for an addiction. You'll exert less effort, more brain-power, more control, and get results faster with much happier satisfaction.

Passionate sex first starts with knowing how to spot sexuality in people. Once found, you'll have the techniques to increase lovemaking thoughts in nonsexual partners, or sustain carnal needs in sexual partners. You'll see, sex exploration will be a lot easier than you thought. From there, building a solid loving relationship comes naturally, automatically, and within your control.

Chapter Eight
What Makes a Healthy Partner?

Feel like you're dangling from an emotional bunge cord? Are you drowning in a relationship that feels wrong? Maybe you've asked yourself, "Why do I keep getting myself into this?" Can't figure it out? Try answering these questions first and then you'll find out why dating doesn't have to be a bummer.

1. Do you have to have an intimate relationship?   YES   NO
2. Do you find yourself attracted to the same type of person?   YES   NO
3. Do you feel paralyzed when partners break up with you?   YES   NO
4. Is it easy to feel what others feel?   YES   NO
5. Do you think living alone is a horrible thing?   YES   NO
6. Do you get "sucked" into relationships where the person has problems?   YES   NO
7. Is it hard to end relationships when you know you should end them?   YES   NO

8. Do you get afraid of going out on dates because of repeating mistakes?   YES   NO

If you circled 8 out of 8 as "Yes," believe me, it's not a perfect score. It means you're doing the two "F's." *Fixing and familiarity.*

If the person needs "fixin," than the relationship feels good, right and familiar. Your helping somebody get better; by pumping them up you're feeling they love you more. And come on, why shouldn't they? You're their coach. You're their cheerleading squad. You're behind them 100%. And that's what feels so familiar about it. We're talking *deja vu.* Just yesterday, or in a relationship you just broke up with, you did the samething. You tried fixing the person so they would want you more. Face it: You're a sucker for wounded deer. That's why you'd make a mistake and slip back in another bad relationship. A relationship built on *What can I do for you now, dear?*

But don't despair. It's no time for pity. You can break this relationship cycle with the snap of your finger and by looking at men *very, very differently.*

It's time to do something really different. Think of your new lover as, say, a new product. Should you buy it? The smart consumer would check it out first. So, that's what you'll do. You'll treat dating like shopping for a car. You'll RATE YOUR DATE. You have to ask yourself, "Is this thing a lemon or will it last?" Go ahead— smell it, kick it's tires, check under the hood, feel the fabric, and really know if this thing has gone sour. That way you can rule out losers and jerks before you give them the key to your heart. And here's the best news of all: It's simple to rate your date.

Lovers take many types. This book willl tell you how to spot each type. For now, consider what makes a *great lover.* They usually fall into three categories. Categories are A, B, & C, and you can compare them in three ways: communication, flexibility, and consistency.

The "A" type can communicate. They're flexible, they're consistent. The "A" type can speak up, put you down or put themselves down. And that's okay. Don't be fooled by their honesty. They can handle all situations; they're a person of their word. Best of all, if "A" makes a promise, "A" follows through.

You'll know when you're dealing with a type B or C person: the red flag goes up, the horn blows, and something feels strange. Or at least it better. B & C types are high risk; they spell doom even before they tell you their names. Here's why:

Type "B" people are never interested in you. They never were. There's a landfill coming out of their mouth. If you're under the avalanche, watch out. For type "B" people, "flexible" is a four-letter word. They look for people to blame; and that means they blame you. B's make a habit of breaking their promises. For example, "B" would be the date who takes you to opening night of *Titanic*. But after arriving and finding it's sold out, watch out. He'll verbally attack you—everything from why didn't you call ahead to reserve tickets, to what took you so long getting ready for the date? And that's not all. He doesn't stop with quickies. He goes for total destruction. No mercy, forget it. He'll make you feel like scum.

"B" is also the one who calls you 100 times a day when you break things off. Not because "B" really loves you, but because *you* should really love "B." How typical, eh? But beware. "B's" are smooth operators. They're slick. And that's what makes them attractive. You see, B's are exciting. They're full of energy—we're talking 800 volts here. Always up, always doing wacky things.

They'll order pizza at 4 in the morning. They'll go swimming in sub-zero temperatures. Weird? Maybe. But it's addictive. And you get hooked in no time. B's sweep you away and make everyday TGIF. Except, of course, when you finally get tired of them being so impulsive. Then it's like, *enough already!* But guess what: They don't get the message. According to "B's," *you're the one who is off base, not them.*

And then there are the "C's." You love this person. Everybody does. That's why "C's" are also addictive. "C's" are marsh- mellows who have a sedative-like effect on you. "C's" make you feel cared for. "C's" are soft fluffy listeners. They listen to everything you say. I mean *everything*. Interrupt? Not them, never. They wouldn't dare. Mums the word. They're afraid if they say what they're thinking, you'll get mad at them. And that would be awful! So instead they smile, look charming, and make you feel loved.

"C" is overflexible. What you want to do is always perfect, and C will do anything for you. Selfish? Not "C." No way. God forbid they should do anything for themselves. They live and breathe for you; your wish is their command. You name it—it's done. And that's all they do: everything is for you. So, the downside is this: You're their life-support-unit. And that can become a drag after a while.

Does this mean if you're dating a "B" or "C" it's time to quit the relationship? Maybe. But only after you confront the person about his behavior and ask the person to change. Sometimes they change, some faster than others. Or, they change just to get you off their back. But that never lasts long. That's why your best approach is to be safe. Your goal is to date "A's."

Focus on finding "A's" even if you feel type "A" people make you nervous. In fact, here's how you really can know you're heading into "A" territory: You meet somebody and instantly think, "I feel uncomfortable around this person, I feel intimidated, they make me feel useless." Don't run. Don't call it quits just yet. You're feeling useless because maybe, just maybe that date doesn't need you to fix him. That date doesn't need for you to be in control. And that date wants to hear your opinions. I know it's strange. And you're probably thinking, *now way!*

But guess again. When you feel "He's way too good for me," backtrack two steps. That means you're dating the *right person. And it feels very differently than when you date the familiar-fixin types.* Be in charge of your decisions.

Know from the get-go who is and who is not a great lover. B's and C's are phenomenal lovers. They soak you up like a sponge underwater. You'll feel yourself sensually absorbed with every erotic cell scintillated. Electrically charged and addictively hungry for another orgasm. You'll be a slave to your body's needs. And, I might add, to their bodies' needs.

Yes, that's right. To *their body needs*. Drowning in passion is one thing. Seduction is another. B's and C's hypnotically charm your into innocent submission. They possess a miraculous knowledge of your erogenous zones and know when your libido is active. Hedonists at heart, they seek pleasures of the flesh over cerebral pleasure. Don't plan on talking about Aristotle with B's and C's.

I don't think so. Not in this world, you won't.

Overwhelmed by their generous loving, it is real easy to lose sight of their pitfalls. And you have to be on your toes to spot bad things in B's and C's. Thank goodness, the rest of the book spell out different types of B's and C's and ways to confront them.

And then there's the "A's." Are also sex-maniacs? Are they jungle animals as well, seeking genital stmulation for survival?

No, not "A's." A's have a different philosophy about sex. It goes like this: *It's nice, and I really like it, but so are other things in life.*

Lovemaking represents one among many ways they achieve personal satisfaction. A's ambitious; they keep busy and advance their skills and minds by socially improving who they know and what they do. Some are presidents of organizations. Other regularly work-out at the spa. But most are into *something. They find incredibly diverse ways to show their talents and do not purely show it through sex.*

That's good news for many of you, looking for a broad-based lover who doesn't think with his or her genitals. A mover and a shaker seems well-rounded, confident and independent. Find this person and you've really discoverd the hidden treasure of gold.

And then, this news may be awful for those of you in touch-withdrawal, who are starving for affection, *A's don't put out? Hell, I don't want them. I'm not settling for a boring person. Already done that, been there, and got plenty of tee-shirts to prove it.*

Boring? Maybe. But that's the ugly compromise for wanting a great lover who doesn't put sex ahead of logic. B's and C's do. They are sex-driven roadhogs who live and die for another chance at blissful orgasm. A's are not like that. They are down-to-Earth, less impulsive and less body-conscious.

So, you choose who fits best for your needs.

Know ahead of time if your date is an "A," "B" or "C." Do this the first time you go out with the person. And save yourself the time, effort and misery of later breakups by thinking wisely today.

Chapter Nine
What Kind of Lover Are You?

Time for you to be real with yourself. Are you an "A," "B" or "C?" Figure this out now before reading on. Take your own temperature first before sticking the thermometer in somebody else's face to see how hot they are.

For a reliable self-exam, you need two things. Honesty and humility. Honesty is sincerely looking at your personality and inner thoughts and not holding back. You'll be tempted to say one thing when you know you mean another. Let your words match your action. Be completely truthful with what is in you. Lies only mask your feeling and interfere with logically solving your curiosity about being a good or bad lover.

Humility? That's an easy one. It's "fess-up" time. Open the floodgates to your vulnerable weak spots and face them one by one. You know flaws exist. Some are hard to miss. Bad habits, forgetfulness, being conceited—there's a host of nasty hang-ups tucked away inside you and hidden from public inspection. You'd die if somebody discovered them; your deadly imperfections. Exposed and humiliated, you'd feel as low as a snail at the bottom of the ocean.

No way. I'm not opening up and showing the real me. Who do you think I am? Some exhibitionist? I can't reveal the real me. I'd be too embarrassed.

Precisely. That's what you and you alone will experience when you answer the following questions:

A great lover is not one who masters the art of lovemaking. That's half the art. The real talent comes in mastering the challenge of making relationships.

Ask yourself if you need these things to make love and answer with Yes or No,

When I make love, I need to…

1. look at pornographic or erotic audio-visual material. YES   NO
2. talk dirty to my partner and get into fantasy with them. YES   NO
3. use vibrators or other electrical devices to heat up the moment. YES   NO
4. masturbate or "prep" myself so I feel horny. YES   NO
5. think about lovemaking hours before actually doing it. YES   NO
6. talk about lovemaking hours, even days before actually doing it. YES   NO
7. put on clothing or costumes that are sexually arousing. YES   NO
8. dare myself or partner to "do it" in public places or at odd times. YES   NO
9. repeat sex shortly after I have an orgasm because it feels so good YES   NO
10. invite other people to watch us or join us with lovemaking. YES   NO

Okay, count your "YES" answers. Five or more (50%) mean you something very good. You're having a love affair with sex. You worship it like the Gods of Olympus. Thoughts obsessively swirl around in your mind about sex, genitals, and who you can achieve orgasm with. Sex urges dominate your waking mind. Outwardly you appear civil and sweet. In church or synagogue you may put on that plastic smile and gently greet friends and relatives with perfunctory kisses on the cheek.

Sure, you can fake it.

But put a stethoscope up to your beating heart and listen carefully to what lies underneath your skin.

I'm horny—can't anyone hear me!

Sure we can. Loud and clear. And so can you. You are the lover who dives deeply into physical flesh for its innately sensual effects. You won't rise to the surface until you feel every ounce of erotic vibration your body can handle. Short of this ecstasy, you feel incomplete, unnurtured, and desperately dissatisfied.

Fully absorbed by passion, you are perfectly in tune with your body needs. Hunger, thirst, pain, grief—all these body emotions get intertwined with sex. Orgasm acts as tranquilizer for rapidly curing annoying physical problems and is a lot cheaper than medicine. Do you, for example, love to have sex when you have…

1. a stomach ache?
2. menstrual cramps?
3. a headache?
4. angry or sad feelings?
5. other body pains?

Sex is top-choice for panacea. Just a dose of orgasm and you feel relieved of physical discomfort and back to your old self.

Compare this sex-thinking with a different type of thinking. Maybe you like sex but are not in its fan-club. Let's find out, shall we? Answer YES or NO for the following. Do you like sex when…

1. there's really nothing else to do and you're bored?
    YES   NO
2. your lover is bugging you and you figure it'll shut them up?
    YES   NO

3. you feel it's your duty as wife, husband or lover?
                    YES NO
4. it's the last priority on your list?
                    YES NO
5. you feel guilty or have been accused of being uncaring?
                    YES NO
6. you think people are having more sex than you are?
                    YES NO
7. you're sure your lover will leave you if you don't?
                    YES NO
8. you know this will get you what you want with your lover.
                    YES NO
9. it means facing your personal hangups or fears about sex?
                    YES NO
10. everything is going "just right" and you feel real confident?
                    YES NO

Okay, tally up your scores. Earned more than half—50% or better? Count again. Are you sure your score is 50% or above?

CONGRATULATIONS. *You hate sex.* That doesn't mean you are a bad lover. Nor does it mean you hate people who are love-capitalists; who spend their waking hours talking or thinking about lovemaking. A low scores means this: sex is not one of your big priorities in life and probably is more of a nuisance for you. It has its place. But not with you.

No matter how proficiently you perform it, lovemaking is put in third class alongside other "do I gotta-do it?" habits such as mowing the lawn or even going to work. Put out of mind, sex is one among many optional activities within your repertoire of recreation. Sometimes you choose it; other times you don't. Selection depends on who you are with and reasons for consenting to sex against your better judgment. You'd always prefer not to do it, but, sure, you're flexible. You'll say "Yes" if really persuaded.

Disinterest in sex largely means you are an extreme "A." You place sensuality in the background of your mind and let other, more exciting challenges preoccupy you. Computer on-line chats, working late at work, even watching sports—all of these past-times electrify your body far more than an orgasm.

Face it; these are your orgasms. You generate extraordinary mental and physical arousal from indulging in stimulating activities that do for you what sex does for others.

And, while, you may still feel all hot and sweaty after a round of tennis or get high from hacking into a computer program, you'll never duplicate the same terrific euphoria by romantically making love.

Chapter Ten
What Is Great Sex?

Sensuous Gods and Goddesses in Cupid's Kingdom are envied as "great lovers." Magically they possessed an inherent alchemy for unleashing passion and perfectly arousing libido pleasures. Their opulent orgies and uninhibited sexual escapades glorified the Grecian lifestyle as a liberated historical period of sexuality. Venerable Greek Gods set the precedent for how citizens behaved. And, like in mythology, citizens frolicked with unrestraining freedom to discover secrets of body stimulation.

Today Greek Gods and mythology are replaced by TV and Hollywood movies. Daily soaps such as *All My Children, General Hospital, Bold and the Beautiful, and One Life to Live* enslave TV viewers to scripted romantic plots slightly imitating reality. In motion pictures, plots take a different twist. Hundreds of romantic plots typically revolve around crime, violence, tragedy and disaster. Blockbuster winners such as *Jackie Brown, Titanic, Tomorrow Never Dies, and Mark of Zorro* dramatically interweave spinal chills of horror with alluring scenes of pure animal magnetism. Death, dying and life-threatening situations seem a potent blend with sexual excitement.

But how much of art duplicates life? Do you really seek a viciously violent partner as a great lover? Do you think being frightened to death induces the best orgasm? Well, some people do. Sado-masochism, or love of pain-infliction, is highly desirable among many sexual entrepreneurs. They are also the thrill-seeking jockeys who push eroticism to death-defying heights. Some use inhalant drugs to induce orgasm. Others tempt asphyxiation to charge up orgasmic release. Abusing the body to experiment powerful sexual gratification may have its momentary benefits. You feel a pulsating rush of adrenaline peaked by a post-seizure-like sedation. And, for sexual adventurers, this cycle is the only way to travel.

But *great sex doesn't require self-abuse*. Great sex is not a measure of giant orgasms and risking life and limb for a shot at Kharma. No, not hardly. Great sex is loving, romantic sex. The type of physical pleasure gained when two caring partners gently touch, kiss, and are consensual. They don't just agree to *have sex, they agree to perform sex from start to finish*.

So, stop being a Juliet to his Romeo. Be you. Be romantic first, and erotic second.

Two wonderful traits of great sex that are easy to develop and delicious to experience are foreplay-afterplay, and showing varieties of affection.

Foreplay and Afterplay

Touch is most invaluable prior to having sex and after you have sex. Before you have sex, or during *foreplay*, breathtakingly graceful touching should be on the outer perimeter of the genitals. *Don't just grab for them jugs. And girls, pinching or tugging at the penis just doesn't prime the pump. You're too rough, too sloppy, and too much in a rush.*

Foreplay-touching is like giving your car a tune-up. Every move is calculated for a total effect. That effect is to lubricate the body so the parts run smoothly and with plenty of fluid. Touching around the genitals, at first, teases the genital and induces stronger arousal. Direct stimulation on the genitals, by contrast, may actually be painful and block arousal. With soft petting comes delicate kissing. Move your lips on your partner's lips like a breeze blowing gently across a room. Don't force a hard-slamming, tongue-thrusting, slobbery kiss where you constantly move your face like a runaway clock pendulum. Sure, that's how the movies depict heavy lovemaking. But ask the actors portraying those love scenes; they'll tell you how real sex is performed—with utmost grace.

Foreplay also has the distinction of being a teaser. It either lures in you in or boots you out of sex. Sweet, passionate steps are a shoe-in for engrossing sex. Lousy form with forceful man-handling will kill the mood. *You're out of luck.*

But no matter how good or bad sex is, after sex is done, you cannot turn over and go to sleep. *Idiot, you just blew the whole experience.* If you didn't know it, let me be the first to inform you: *Sex is not the act of fornicating and achieving orgasm. Any animal or insect can do that. Sex is a fuller experience with a beginning, middle and end. And don't go forgetting the end part, or you won't get sex again.*

The finishing part is called *afterplay*. Afterplay stereotypically is pictured with a couple laying side by side smoking a cigarette, reflecting on their sexual conquests. You hear them ask, "Was it good for you?" and the partner replies affirmatively, "Yes, my love, it was." I know, it's corny but that's how the stereotype appears.

In real life afterplay is not as glamorous. Couples who complete intercourse and mutually achieve climax are really tired. They already had a busy morning, afternoon, or evening and are ready for slumberland. A shot of orgasm followed by muscular dilation knocks them out in a hurry. They may not do it intentionally but are sound asleep within minutes of rolling over.

How can afterplay be embellished if you're so tired? I'll tell you how. You can do it in three ways. First, don't surprise your partner. Tell him or her ahead of time you want afterplay. Describe exactly what you have in mind; holding each other; more kissing, resting together while talking, or watching TV. Be upfront with your intentions and receptive to your partner's input including even negative opinions against wanting afterplay. Talk it through quietly with the goal of *some compromise.*

Second, make it a routine. Sex frequency may be low, but make sure afterplay follows every rare occasion. Consistency creates the sincere impression you really love your partner and want time with him or her after the fireworks display.

Third, duplicate the afterplay in any other situation where you are not having sex. Like, for example, at night when you sit together on the couch watching TV. Kiss, hug, softly touch, and rest silently in each other's arms undisturbed by noises or competing activities. Afterplay can fit into any private moment, making it more romantic and serene. As you turn many parts of your life into mini-afterplay episodes, you're showing how sex is wonderful, but not the only way to thoroughly enjoy your partner.

Okay "touch" areas

What is "safe" to touch? Genitals? *God no!* Shoulders? Maybe. Or, is there a general safety zone around the body that partners usually say "YES" to? Sometimes. Every person is different. Let's assume you're relationship is okay except for sex. Then, you'll find sensitive areas. Partners may be quiet about these physical prime spots, but their area "45" does exist. You will be able to find the base where they hide their own exterterrestial secrets. By contrast, say you're on a first date with your partner. Can you rely on those same prime spots for touch? NO! And don't be fresh; don't be Jack who jumped over the candlestick or you'll get your self burned.

Be careful, calibrated, selective, and know the good and bad effects of physical touching. Begin with safe touch zones.

Safe touch zones. Even the Cape Crusader himself doesn't slobber over victims he saves. Touch is reserved for unique opportunities. You touch *for a reason and the reason is not always to get sex. Touch only leads to sex if touching is done right.* For ongoing partners who don't want sex, touch is a like the mail delivery truck. It carries the mail. The mail are your tender, empathic words and caring remarks. As you speak, touch slips its way through the cracks from your space to your partner's space. That space consists of an area extending from their foreheads to their shoulders and including their hands. Stay out of the chest-zone. It's off-limits!

Touch only those parts unassociated in any way with foreplay or sexual stimulation. Touch the:
 · Forehead
 · Face
 · Left or right shoulders
 · Left or right arms and hands

For new dates, confine touching only to hands and shoulders. Keep a solid distance away while touching. Close touching feels invasive. Never violate restricted body zones near or around the chest or below the waist no matter how innocent your intentions. If you do, you pervert, two things happen. First, you're drilling for oil in a dry spot. No way you're sexual advances will win you a one-nighter or even a repeat date. Second, you're signaling a message loud and clear that you're not interested in this partner unless he or she puts out.

But, hey! After I spend this amount of money on a date, I expect this partner to reciprocate a little and show me a good time. Isn't that the fair thing to do?

Sure, if you're a jerk. Sex is not a Hallmark thank-you card. Partners just don't give-it-away for free because you've been peachy toward them. *Sex, no matter who it's with, requires some degree of trust and comfort. Even one-night stands require both partners to show some respect to one another.* So, on first dates, I suggest you restrict your touching only to hands and arms. No farther up the anatomical scale. And keep a relative distance while touching so your partner doesn't think you've pressed them into a corner and are mentally raping them.

So, now that you got the touch-zone longitude, latitude and altitude right, let's consider velocity. Pace is everything. Fast, rushed and rigid touches feel like an animal is groping for food. *If you're that hungry for sex, masturbate before going out with your partner. Otherwise, cool your jets.*

Touch is a soft, delicate, and slow process of reaching your hand gently into your partner's touch zone and keeping it there for 2 to 4 seconds. That's it. *Now, get it the Hell out of there.* Remove that sucker before he or she thinks you're a priest giving them last rights. Prolonged touching also makes you look like a blood-sucking leach; you're draining every ounce of energy from them the longer your hand stays affixed onto their hands.

You can take your hand away. You'll survive. Believe me, you will. After you touch a hand, a shoulder, even a face, take a break. A small recess. Don't be in a hurry to rush back to the ice-cream vendor for another popsicle. Re-group your thoughts. And put the breaks on urges. You may feel that touching your partner made good headway; now he or she really knows I care and I want them to further feel my passion for them.

Good, you're on the right path. But don't wear out the path or you'll never find your way to their bodies again. If you're feeling touch was effective, it means they did, too. Let them savor the feeling before you go back for another dose of feeling good.

Patiently wait until your partner gives you a sign—any sign—that your touching meaningfully induced caring feelings for you. They'll show this by smiling, touching you back, or literally thanking you for being compassionate (e.g., "Thanks for caring"). This certifies your touching was on target and doesn't need a repeat flight to its destination.

You did well the first time. Don't be greedy and double the pleasure just for kicks.

So remember, moderate sex is not euphoric. Power-house eroticism gets you in trouble. You become addicted and lose your mental faculties. Absorbed forever in fantasy, pleasure loses its reality and becomes an illusion. You pretend you're flying in sensual space without a care in the world. Trouble is, no matter how high you fly, what goes up always crashes down. Very fast. And really hard. Sex for sex only is like crashing down..without a parachute. A nose-dive into hard cement—all for thinking sex was all-important.

Well, it's not. And healthy relationships depend on lovers who treat sex like food. Eat a good meal when food is served; but don't over-indulge and know when you're full. Otherwise, you get a food overdose. A sex overdose is similar. Over-doing sex is bordering on addiction that ruins your life and blemishes love. Love turns into a perversion.

So, as you read and re-read this book, remember your goal is simple. Treat sex as you would a precious diamond. Respect and admire it, being delicate with its fragile and unique structure. Treat it with dignity and especially the partner who has made this sexual diamond a privilege for you to have and enjoy.

About the Author

Douglas Ruben

Dr. Douglas Ruben is a family and addictions psychologist and media consultant. He is author, co-author and "scriptdoctor" of over 40 books, two screenplays, and 100 professional articles. Seen on DONAHUE and TV and radio coast-to-coast, his recent self-help books include *Bratbusters: Say Goodbye To Tantrums & Disobedience; No More Guilt: 10 Steps To a Shame-Free Life; Avoidance Syndrome; Family Recovery; 60 Seconds To Success; One Minute Secrets To Feeling Great;* and *Forever Sober.* He also wrote the blueprint for other authors with *Your Public Image: TV, Radio, and Print Media in Clinical Practice,* and *Writing for Money in Mental Health.* Remaining books are scholarly for college libraries. Dr. Ruben is in private practice and president of Best Impressions International Inc, a media consulting firm.

CPSIA information can be obtained
at www.ICGtesting.com
Printed in the USA
LVHW111012241220
675077LV00013B/69